CH00869356

In the Blink of an Eye –
Reborn

Peter Coghlan

www.petercoghlan.com

Copyright © 2018 Peter Coghlan

All rights reserved

ISBN-13: 978-1727145595

ISBN-10: 1727145593

Cover design by Ivan Longland - www.apaganza-art.com

FOREWORD

I've been involved with the care of stroke patients for more than 20 years and have witnessed the full range of human emotions, tragedies and triumphs, experienced by stroke survivors and their loved ones. I have frequently shared in the grief, frustration and pain, and still find the task of delivering bad news distressing. There are however, some shining moments of glorious and spectacular recovery; Peter's story is one of them. So often the media describes a patient's recovery as "against all odds" with the doctors pessimistically quoted as saying, "You'll never walk again," or "You will need to go to a nursing home." Whilst some reports of Peter's story have included such phrases, they were never from me; in fact, my interactions with Peter have always been the exact opposite.

Peter was admitted to the ward in mid-2011. I hadn't been involved directly with his initial care but was soon aware of his circumstances and what had happened. I had long been a proponent of mechanical thrombectomy for severe stroke due to clotting within the large arteries of the brain and have been involved with this therapy since the mid-1990s. It took until 2015 for this approach to be finally proven as a technique, so attempts to use it prior to that date were certainly regarded as 'cutting edge', or possible a little 'cowboyish'. In situations like Peter's, though, the decision-making is relatively simple - a very fit, active young patient facing death or severe disability. In my view, there was no hesitation in trying everything. Other clinicians might have been more conservative, particularly prior to the publication of the 2015 data, for fear of leaving Peter alive and facing devastating disability. In any case, Peter was transferred from a peripheral hospital in the middle of the night, to the major tertiary hospital, and one of interventional neuroradiology fellows, in conjunction with my colleague, made some urgent decisions, and proceeded to mechanically extract a lengthy clot from Peter's basilar artery during the early hours of the morning.

In this book, Peter describes in graphic detail the horror of awakening in the intensive care unit, and the gradual realization of his situation; the 'locked-in syndrome' (LIS). In summary, individuals with LIS find their fully active mind, trapped in a completely paralysed body, usually due to a stroke affecting the middle section of the brainstem; a critical section of neural tissue connecting the brain to the upper spinal cord. Typically, all four limbs are paralysed, and the nerves controlling speech, swallowing and breathing are affected. The patient is unable to speak, and observers may assume they are comatose and not aware of the surrounding environment. Communication can sometimes be established through eye-blinking, and other subtle facial movements. One of the most famous cases is described in the book, and movie, "The Diving Bell and the Butterfly" by Jean-Dominique Bauby.

Shortly after Peter was transferred to the neurology ward, I was formally asked to consult on his case, particularly to assess his suitability for transfer to the neurology ward of the rehabilitation hospital, where I also worked. Despite seeing hundreds of stroke patients each year, I had only been involved with four cases of locked-in syndrome (who had survived) due to stroke before I met Peter; but this was more than most of my colleagues. Two early patients remain highly dependent, one in a nursing home, the other with full time family care at home. Another patient had been spectacularly saved by thrombectomy more than 24 hours after symptom onset and progressed through rehabilitation quite rapidly. I presented his case at a meeting to highlight what could be done. I contrasted his outcome with another patient who didn't do so well initially, but ultimately underwent a long rehabilitation process with some gains, and returned home, and resumed a productive life. She came tantalisingly close to walking but, due to a number of issues, couldn't quite get back on her feet. Around the time that Peter came in, I was feeling particularly enthusiastic about neuroplasticity and rehabilitation. The famous book written by Norman Doige, 'The Brain That Changes Itself', was receiving a lot of popular press, and I'd just heard him give a public lecture, affirming many of the basic principles that I'd been working with for years. Although it wasn't really new knowledge for me, it was inspiring and exciting for the public and patients to have some hope provided. In the book, Doige describes the recovery process of a doctor's father who suffered a severe brainstem stroke. 'hat inspirational description included a phase where the patient crawled like an infant in the process of re-learning to walk. I felt "fired up' by these descriptions and eager to apply this the next time I had a suitable patient with LIS.

When I carefully reviewed the details of Peter's case, I was quietly optimistic. His MRI showed that the damage to a critical portion of the brainstem known as the pons was incomplete. An important few millimeters of tissue known as the corticospinal tract seemed to be relatively intact. This region is the 'wiring' which transmits electrical signals from the brain to the body. It's incredible what difference a few millimeters of damage, one way or the other, can make. What I saw on the scan gave me hope, but what I saw in Peter when I met and examined him gave me even more hope. I saw a fit, relatively young man who was determined. I knew it was vital to get through to him, and make him understand there was hope, and I tried to do this when I met him. I was surprised to later read in his first book, how great the impact of my decision to get him into the rehabilitation hospital was; from my side of the bed there was no doubt that was the only thing to do. It's easy to forget how the things doctors say and do really stand out in the minds of patients. I had to be realistic, though, and warn him there was plenty of work to do, and that it would be a long road.

So, Peter's rehabilitation journey began. Typically, I'd visit the rehabilitation hospital once or twice a week and attend a detailed meeting where the nurses and the therapy staff would give their reports on patients' progress. The highlight for me was seeing patients in normal clothes in the gymnasium working with the physiotherapists, rather than being stuck in a bed wearing pyjamas. I think that environment is crucial because it can be very inspiring and motivating, as well as tough. Patients get to see others in action as well, at different stages in rehabilitation, and with different levels of age and disability. Sometimes a sense of friendly competition arises; other times, disappointment can be the result. The team clinical psychologist has a crucial role to help guide patients and their relatives through the "bumps in the road", that the long journey of rehabilitation must take when a patient has profound neurological injury like the LIS. Peter certainly had 'bumps' to face, including at least two frightening episodes of pneumonia. But Peter overcame the challenges to walk out of 'Shents'. The video of that still makes me cry!

There was much more to follow for Peter after discharge from inpatient rehabilitation; in some ways the intensity of his efforts accelerated. Around this time, I was quite enthusiastic about long distance running, and a member of the West Australian Marathon Club. Another member named Daryl Howel has cerebral palsy and has famously competed in marathons and ultra-marathons around the world. This made me wonder what Peter could do, and somewhere along the line I challenged him to join me in the Perth City to Surf, initially planning to participate in the 4km walk. Peter's determination of course quickly changed the target to the full 12km event. It was a wet and cold day when Peter and I completed the course, which was being deconstructed as we slowly covered the distance, but a glorious achievement and milestone for Peter. A couple of years later we went even further, walking 16km in the John Hughes Big Walk. On a beautiful clear day, I think Peter could have walked forever!

There are many other things that Peter has done including his generous support and help for other patients, and there are many more great things in his future. Peter's inspiration also helps me show up for work every day. Stroke medicine is demanding. Most days I interact with patients and families who are going through the worst thing that has ever happened to them. The stress, grief and shock associated with stroke is enormous, and I admit that despite all my years of working in the field it still sometimes overwhelms me and gets me down. When it does though, there is no better way for me to find inspiration than to think of Peter Coghlan.

David Blacker, MB BS, FRACP
Neurologist and Stroke Physician, Sir Charles Gairdner Hospital
Clinical Professor of Neurology, University of WA
Medical Director, Perron Institute for Neurological and Translational Science

Chapter 1

*Six o'clock in the afternoon, 21st March 2011.
Another summer's day in Perth. Another barbecue with
family and friends. Me, Ted, Jade, on the terrace downing a
couple of ciders, talking, laughing, enjoying a smoke, then
me a bit tired, feeling fuzzy, going for a nap.*

*Awake confused and agitated, slurring my words,
remembering the fuzziness earlier in the day, the
temporary blindness when my eyes went fuzzy with stars:
"Think I've had a stroke." Everyone sitting by the bar - Jade,
Dave, Ted, Sean, Julia, my sister Vicky – are really
concerned, trying to get me walking, to walk a straight line
down the garden. Then comes the vomiting and my mind
starts whizzing – but, hey, it's cool, it's cool: "I'll be okay,
just a cup of tea and a piece of toast, I'll be okay." Hoping
it'll pass over me like it did before, but my words are
slurring badly now, the old ticker's racing. Jade and Vicky
are on the internet, seeing what's wrong. "Better get you to
hospital!" says Jade, trying not to sound worried, "just in
case."*

*Now things really kick off! I'm in the car and it's
racing down the freeway and all I see is lights, lights,
flashing lights, hear Jade saying: "Stay with me! Stay with
me, Pete!" Dave's driving, foot on the floor, holding me
upright in the front while Jade tries to steady me from the
back, holding my shoulders while I'm throwing up all over
the place, and she's pleading: "Stay with me! Stay with me!"
Racing, racing down the freeway, over 120km per hour but
it's too late, I'm losing it, going limp, and Jade's still yelling,
but louder now: "Stay with me, Pete! We're nearly there!
Stay with me!"*

*We've stopped at Joondalup hospital. I'm being pulled
out of the car then I imagine that two big blokes are lifting
me up, talking about what's happened: "It's just genetics,
mate." And suddenly they disappear and I'm being wheeled
along a corridor, must be hospital, but just don't know*

anymore, don't know anything anymore. God, please help me!

Sitting upright in a chair in a big open room with a needle stuck in my arm. Lungs bursting, fighting for breath, retching, puking, heart going nineteen to the dozen with loud, heavy, ominous thuds. Helpless, lifeless, witless with fear. "He's not had anything!" cries Jade, frustration and sheer panic rising in her voice. Three times they ask, wasting time and oxygen; three times she answers, "He's not had ANYthing!" Wish I HAD taken something, then at least I'd know what's wrong, but no one ends up this bad after two halves of cider. Must have been that knock on the head, yes that's it! While I was laying storm pipes earlier, standing to stretch, I cracked my head on a piece of concrete sticking out of the sandy trench! It knocked me for six, smashed into the back of my skull. But me being a hard nut never thought to get it checked out. Jade's been given a form to fill in while my sister Vicky starts banging on the window, frantically yelling for a doctor. Nurse walks off, people passing by, ignoring me. Maybe they're embarrassed because now I'm going into spasm, arms twisting in ways they were never meant to go, shaking like an egg-whisk on full speed. Maybe I'm not here at all; maybe it's just a bad dream - yes, that's it, that must be why I'm slipping into the blackness.

Joondalup A+E

Vicky really kicked off – so, no doubt realising I've not got DTs or OD'd on ecstasy, the doctors finally arrive, but now I'm shuddering, shaking so violently the only thing they can do is put me out. Oblivion.

Sir Charles Gairdner – Intensive Care Unit

Weird place, coma. Dark room filled with smoke, me on a bed, helpless, limp and my head feels so, so heavy, I can't lift it from the pillow, not even a millimetre. Jade,

Mum, Vicky and Maria, they're here but, hey, something's not right. THEY'RE not right, not looking at me, expressionless, soundless, weird A voice telling them to join in – some kind of 'entertainment' it says.

Middle of the room, an enormous Ottoman-type sofa, bright blue and circular and the voice is now telling the girls to take their clothes off. What? Here? Funny kind of hospital, this! Can't believe what I'm hearing, can't bear what I'm seeing. Is this really happening? Now blokes, loads of them, all standing around, waiting their turn with the girls on the Ottoman, and me – karate brown belt and jiu-jitsu enthusiast, ex-soldier - just lying here not able to move, not able to make them stop! Wanting to shout, scream out loud yet powerless to speak, crying inside with pain because these zombies are having an orgy, pleasuring themselves with women I care about, and one of them is Jade.

Jade. The one! The only! I knew it from the first. Tumbling, dark-brown hair, a smile to split your heart open and a smile to put the sun to shame - that's if you ever saw the sun in Derbyshire. Move over Mills & Boon.

Trying not to look. Trying to blot it out. It's not real, can't be real, I know my Jade! Suddenly the girls have gone and I'm in this purple room, some kind of brothel, with 8 other people and it's my turn to be a slave, to lie back and take it. I'm desperate to get out, but I just can't move, my head is so very, very heavy.

Vaguely, I'm aware of my friend Dan De Silva arriving while I'm still in ICU. He's come straight from the airport to see me but they won't let him in. "Carry me out of here, Dan! Please, please get me out of here!" But they won't let him in! I'm a prisoner!

What I need is distraction, yes, to take myself away, far away from tubes and hospitals and doctors and the rancid stench of vomit and fear. Back to reality, back to the familiar, back to the known. If only I could lift my head off the pillow.

Just like the cobbler's children with holes in their shoes, being the son of a copper was no guarantee of good behaviour. From the moment I burst into the world on the 5th July 1977, sucking in huge lungfuls of oxygen to fuel my ear-piercing shrieks for attention, I've been a bit of a tearaway. Actually, I've been a *lot* of a tearaway, so much so it's a wonder I didn't end up in jail. Can't even make the usual excuse of a miserable childhood, never having been bullied, abandoned or abused in any way.

On the contrary, I was given the best upbringing ever by my loving parents - Phil Coghlan, a policeman, and his wife Anne, a qualified nurse - in the pleasant rural areas of Stockport, near Manchester. My childhood was idyllic with sunshine holidays, family celebrations and all the usual mischief small boys get up to. When I was 4 years old, our family was increased by a new arrival, Victoria, my little sister and the closest family member I've ever had.

Vicky and I grew up not just as siblings but as real friends, sharing each other's problems and secrets; you know, the ones no teenage kid ever wants parents to find out about. But Vicky and I - we were close – I felt it was my duty and privilege to protect her for the whole of our lives.

I wasn't perfect, of course. Especially at school where, as far as I was concerned, reading and writing were the pits! I couldn't wait to leave the education system and get into the big, wide world to do all the things I enjoyed. As soon as I was tall enough to stare Stallone in the kneecap, I took up martial arts, graduating seamlessly through the coloured belt system with surprisingly little bruising in the process. My first love was Shotokan Karate, a very demanding form of self-defence, calling for intense discipline and high levels of physical fitness. Even then, I wasn't satisfied. After achieving my brown belt, I took up yet another challenge - Jiu-jitsu, which I stuck at for three to four years.

In common with most teenage lads, girls were never far from my mind and me and my three closest pals in Whaley Bridge - Dan Hodson, Matt Storey and Gavin Hill - made a formidable trio, sneaking the odd pint of beer and tarting ourselves up for nights spent chatting up the local talent. All in all, we didn't do a bad job of it either, considering none of us were what you'd call streetwise. None of us had ever ventured far from our small village surroundings.

I seem to be in some kind of hell and there's something really, really disturbing going on. I'm being raped, at least I think I am - but no, no, it's just an enema, a tube full of water, and it's being pumped into my rear until I foul myself while Dad and Vicky are watching, laughing at me and pointing at the mess. Of course, it isn't really happening, they're not here, not really, only in my mind. Reality is Auntie May, shaking her head with a pained, sad look on her face: "Such a shame, so young, so young." But then, she can't see those other people, strange people with no bodies - just massive heads on sticks. Seriously! Human heads on plastic lollipop sticks. They terrify me! Far nicer are the miniature men, two of them, barely three inches tall in tiny black suits and matching blue shirts. I don't mind them. I think they may be brothers, two kindly little souls who tuck me in, wipe my brow and pull my covers up around my neck to keep me warm. Daft, maybe, but in this half-lit, nightmare world, I'll take any comfort I can get – however small. Wish I was a kid again, a cheeky kid running wild.

Me and my mates were bound to get into trouble some day. Only with us it was *every* day, especially in the summer. On one of our treks through the bracken-strewn hills and rich green forests of Derbyshire's High Peak we came across a caravan. You know the sort – dumped in the corner of a field, moulded over green, windows blackened with age. But for young kids like us, this was a real find, a den, our own special hideaway.

"Best clean it up a bit first," said Carl. Carl Farrell, whose Dad was a policeman like mine, was a local lad I hung out with right back to babyhood, liked things tidy. So we got started, me with a ragged old rag, Carl blowing the dust off surfaces and choking himself in the process, although neither of us tackled the cobwebs; that's 'cos we were both terrified of spiders but much too macho to admit it. Then I had a *brilliant* idea.

"Let's try this," I suggested eagerly.

Rooting through my backpack I eventually found what I was looking for – a full box of matches, packed away for just such an occasion, in the cupboards a half rusted tin of easy start, 'it was on'..... This was a stunt I'd been dying to try since seeing it in a James Bond movie. After shaking the can vigorously, I lit a match with one hand and with my other hand pressed the spray button on the Easy Start can. Hey Presto! The moisture burst into flames, which in turn ignited the cobwebs along with all their resident creepy-crawlies. Unfortunately, they ignited the curtains too.

"OMG!" I said, looking sheepishly at Carl, and paused to consider the effects. Carl nodded understandingly. I'd swear the lad was psychic!

"Ohhhh shiiiit!" I yelled, and we hurled ourselves out of the caravan, now engulfed in flames, and had only sprinted a few yards before the whole vehicle exploded into an enormous fireball. If we'd had any sense, we'd have legged it there and then before the fire engines arrived, but we were so fascinated by our home-made inferno, we didn't think to run until the farmer grabbed us each by the ear.

It won't move. My head won't move. It's like a massive demolition ball, a dead weight dropped from a great height, smashed into the pillow where it now slumps helplessly, too heavy to move. I try to raise it, even an inch,

13

but no. It won't budge. Nothing will budge. The only thing moving in my body is saliva, drools of it, dribbling freely down my chin, my neck, my sheets, everywhere, litres and litres and litres of the stuff.

The caravan escapade cost me a packet – a year's pocket-money in compensation...plus I had to help out at the farm to make amends! "Make the punishment fit the crime," my Dad always said, but it didn't put me off. Some folk never learn do they? My next trick was more ambitious. Aided by my mate Peter Evison, I set fire to a whole row of 'House for Sale' signs, an act of pure vandalism. Everyone blamed it on turf wars between rival estate agents, a mythical feud which many locals believe to this day.

On another occasion, I almost combusted my best friend, Dan, by placing lighted cigarettes between each of his fingers as he lay unconscious on a sofa, after a particularly heavy acid session in some house party in Disley. No malice intended, of course and, thanks to his sense of humour and amazing tolerance, our friendship has remained Titanium. Looking back, this not-so-latent pyromania no doubt influenced my decision to live in Australia – all those barbecues!

Jade's here. Not sure how, not sure when, just know she's here. But that's Jade, always with me, always, right from the beginning. And she knows that I'm here too. She bends over to whisper in my ear, voice kind and gentle: "Pete? Can you hear me? If you can hear me, blink." And I blink. Afraid she'll think it's just a natural tic, I blink again, harder this time, hard as I can. That's done the trick, now Jade knows I can hear; she can talk to me and I can answer her! Thank God! I'm not alone anymore! Jade's with me, stepping in, sharing the nightmare.

My Dad never knew the half of it! When I wasn't blowing up caravans, me and Carl were crawling through sewage pipes underground, exploring empty buildings, whatever mischief we could find that we had a fair chance of getting away with. In all honesty, it was verging on criminal at times, like when stealing chocolate from the local newsagents. This was a regular practice until I got caught red-handed with the 'loot' - over 200 Mars Bars in one summer! Don't ask me why, as I never ate them! Maybe it was just to irritate my Dad, being the rebellious little so'n'so I was!

Head still heavy; still glued to the pillow by my own mucus and spit dripping remorselessly from my ever-drooling mouth. My mouth and jaw seem to sag to one side, drooped in a permanent downward sneer.

Whether it was coincidental or a subconscious act of rebellion, I can't say, but when Dad was with the Drug Squad for a spell, I rolled home delirious after eating magic mushrooms, picked and dried in a shoe box from Disley Golf Course a few weeks prior! One of their effects was to dilate my pupils, turning my eyes coal black, giving me a demonic look which I tried to blame on beer. Of course there was the usual lecture but, as usual, I wasn't listening. All I could see was Dad creating trails of technicolour rainbows as he waved his hands about; me enjoying the light show while he ranted and raved. Omg, he was so mad that night! I must have been nuts but, back then, a mushroom tea and the strains of Black Sabbath on a Saturday afternoon were my idea of heaven! "WHAT IS THIS THAT STANDS BEFORE ME?!" Ozzy ringing around my head.

Getting arrested, of course, was purely a matter of time. Yet, when it did happen, it wasn't for arson but for mooning at staff at a MacDonald's take-away! Police officers on duty were not amused, even less so on learning my father was a cop. "You should know better then, shouldn't you?" was their only retort, refusing to make any allowances for my family connections, bunging me and my mates into a squad van...

Locked-in for the very first time!

Chapter 2

Sir Charles Gairdner Hospital - Ward G51

Awake again, still in the nightmare, trying to look around but eyes won't move, not properly - just up and down. The 'ottoman' incident was obviously not real, just the product of a damaged mind. It must be, because my eyes don't work, don't focus. I can't see. Desperately, I scan the ceiling, trying to swivel my eyes, to make things out, to pinpoint something, anything. But all I can see is ceiling and dark, unfriendly shadows. Can't hear either. Not properly. Sound comes and goes like a badly tuned radio, from high-pitched buzzing to faint, hollow echoes; from muffled whispering to urgent, anguished cries. None of my senses are working; just fluctuate from one extreme to another.

In my visual fog, I can just make out a blue ball hanging from my chest, some sort of monitor, I guess. Neck moves slightly so I'm turning, desperately wrenching my two-ton-weighted head from side to side trying to increase my range of vision, trying to speak, but my tongue doesn't work and this is the scariest thing because I want to know what's happened and there's no way I can ask if I'm going to be okay. So I do the only thing I can. I cry. The incessant dribble competes with hot salt tears splashing from my face onto the pillow, until my eyes smart and my ears start itching. I've been crying like this since I first regained consciousness, so I'm getting really good at it. Too good.

At least my sight is improving. I can just make out a care plan on the wall with a makeshift picture of me in a wheelchair with a list of needs on it, and it scares the hell out of me, thinking this is forever, thinking this is my future and this is how they see me. Too sudden, too stark. The horror of going to bed then waking up from a coma and seeing that wheelchair is scarier than the scariest, scary movie. I'm trying to read the care plan, to find out what's going on, but have got double vision and all I can fix on is a

17

sign in the bathroom: "Please don't put Terry wipes in the toilet. It will block. Thanks."

Another agonising twist, this time to the right. An electric fan is whirring and I see a window, but there's a crane outside, blocking out the light slightly, There's also a TV with a mirror below it but I only want to see myself, and in my mind I'm twisting but the body doesn't budge. It just won't budge. Oh God help me! Now I'm crying again and the tears are trickling into my ears and down my neck, wet and cold and trickling and as impossible to control as the rest of me. Someone comes in and starts drying my eyes and then she (I think it's a 'she') starts telling me where I am and what has happened.

"You're in hospital, Pete... you've just had an operation, so you're bound to feel groggy for a while."

She left something out! 'Will I be all right?' I want to know. Please tell me! Will I be all right?!

Now she's shoving a tube up my nose and giving me drugs – aspirin maybe – then some liquid food through a drip. The nurse calls it Jevity and tells me it's packed with goodness, everything my body needs. It looks like some kind of mocha drink and comes in a tin. I watch as the nurse empties the tin into a bottle which she then hangs upside down so it starts dripping slowly through my nose and into my belly. Then I keep watching as it drips, drips and drips for hours, trying to remember things, to think of happy times, trying to keep from going mad. But then, memories hurt too. Trophies I've won in karate, marching on manoeuvres, even simple things like walking in fields with my dog Cody, things I once took for granted but may never do again.

"Well, you won't be doing THAT again!" Dad was less than sympathetic over my latest stunt, putting it down to idleness and sheer boredom. "Okay, party's over, time to get a job!" Ah well, everyone needs to work for a living and I wasn't averse to that.

Before joining the police, my dad had been a carpenter and joiner and liked to keep his hand in from time to time, using his skills for friends and colleagues. He often took me with him on these jobs, making me feel grown up and wanting to be a tradesman just like him.

Then again, I'd set my heart on being a soldier, no doubt due to all those Rambo movies and the pretend war games I loved playing in the woods, me and Carl camouflaged by muddy knees and faces. But, as always, Dad had the right idea.

"Learn a trade first," he advised, "Doesn't matter which one you choose, but with a good trade under your belt, you'll never want for work."

Naturally, I moaned about it at the time, thinking Dad was just putting obstacles in my way, but with hindsight I came to realise how valuable this advice was and it's certainly stood me in good stead. Though still determined to join the army, I went to college where I learned to be a bricklayer. After all, people would always need houses, ey!

And why should I rush into anything when life as a teen was proving such a blast!

Drip, drip, drip! Time has lost its meaning. All I can do is lie here, counting the seconds which turn into minutes which turn into hours, punctuated only by the nurses coming in to grind my medication. They do this in a mortar and pestle like in science at school, and then the powder's put in a syringe and injected up my nose through a tube that's permanently fixed. Some nurses are really good, chatty and pleasant, but one or two act as though I didn't exist, not even bothering to look me in the eye, as though I was just some object, an animal carcass with no feelings. But I CAN feel; I DO feel; I feel everything, from the aching of my head to the tortuous spasms in my twisted hands and feet.

All I have, all I can use to distract me from this hell are memories and even these taunt me, confronting me with the boy I used to be, Peter Coghlan, the copper's kid who could never keep still, the likely lad who was always on the go.

"Cogs, you muppet!" yelled Dan. He had a point. Who but me would get us stranded in the middle of nowhere with no breakdown cover, this in the days before mobile phones. Me, Dan and the rest of the lads had been heading for a burger bar in town when the car ran out of fuel – hardly surprising as, with me being broke most of the time, it had to keep going on petrol fumes. So there we were, stuck.

"Ey up, Dan look! There's a farmhouse." Outside the tumbledown rural dwelling was a cement mixer. Surely there'd be enough fuel in it to get us back to civilisation. "I'll nick a bit."

Dan, of course, was all for it and leapt out of the car, willing and eager to help as always, switching to stealth mode!

Just one problem. "Damn! I've no petrol can!"

"Not to worry," said Dan. "This'll do." He'd found an old plastic cup from MacDonald's - it must have been rolling around for months on the floor of my car.

"It's even got its own siphon!" Sure enough, there was a straw in the cup which Dan waved above his head triumphantly.

A few seconds later, with a few cupfuls of stolen fuel in my tank, we were on our way, the car wheezing and spluttering worse than an asthmatic donkey. And no wonder – the 'hot' fuel we'd siphoned was farmers' red diesel which completely wrecked my engine! But at least it got us home.

Lack of money was a constant problem, although it never stopped us having a laugh. When I had my own (extremely dingy) flat, life didn't start until 1am after the pubs had shut. That's when all my mates rolled in to cheer me up, bottles in hand, and started eating toast between puffs of funny stuff. "Right, Cogs!" they'd say, by now completely sozzled. "We're sick of you moaning about having no money and your rubbish flat! Get your trainers on!"

"How about a spot of gardening first?" The rest of us looked at each other. Funny how everyone seemed to be swaying from side to side – but whether that was due to their lack of balance or my inability to focus properly, I'll never know. With no more ado, we all trooped into the neglected, empty garden and started digging it over. "Hang on a tick!" said Dan, "It's missing something." "What's that?" I asked. "A bench. Yes, it definitely needs a bench!"

Ten minutes later, we were running back up the road with a bench we'd found, unloved and unwanted, outside our local pub, four of us holding a corner and trying to stay upright – almost impossible to do for laughing. Matt and Gav didn't help much either, trying to sit on the thing as we were carrying it, while me and Dan at the rear end kept tripping over the legs of the bench.

"Watch the Plod be round the next corner!" I shouted. "We'd be done for speeding!" "AND drunken driving!" chortled Dan, now nicely wasted on Stella lager.

Plonked in the middle of my stamp-sized patch of grass, the bench looked rather boring – and lonely. "Could do with some greenery," I suggested. "Just to soften the effect." So off we set again, the six of us, looking for anything we could use to titivate my little plot of paradise. At the last count, we had seven conifers, a rhododendron, a few other plants I didn't know the names of – and a very cheerful-looking garden gnome.

Wake up with a wet pillow. It's always wet. Just as my hands are always hurting. I can hear Jade in the corridor, whispers of her voice. She and my Mum talking to the doctor (think she's called Dr Steel) and she's trying to explain what's happened to me. Seems I had a clot on my brain; it had to be removed through my femoral artery, whatever that is. Can only get snatches of their conversation; words like basilar, pons and, more frighteningly, 'vegetative' and 'locked-in'. When I hear these terms, their voices get lower and I can tell they don't want me to hear them. Only they don't know if I CAN hear, except for Jade: "He CAN understand, I know he can! He blinks!" Suddenly, I'm struck with the most horrific thought of all – maybe the doctors think I'm dead! Maybe I AM dead! Maybe that's why, that's why I keep thinking back, back through my life.

Looking back, life might have turned out differently had I buckled down to college instead of bunking off for days at a time. As it was, teenage testosterone, my mates and the lure of the local pub seemed a far better option than lectures and training sessions; besides, after two years laying bricks, I was pretty bored of college and still hankered for a life in the army where I'd become a well-disciplined, exemplary soldier of daring courage, in my home "Cheshire Regiment."

One lunch time, I sauntered into the Army Careers Centre for more information about being a dog handler or driver. "Yeah, yeah," said the soldier on duty, all pleasant and positive and telling me I could go where I wanted when I got to my battalion but....."I'll have to get you in through the infantry," he said and me, of course, being wet behind the ears, said "OK," and promised to persuade my folks to come to the office.

I went home that day worried and scared of what my dad would say but knowing it had to be done if I wanted the chance of an army career. Besides, I could see all this bumming around was getting me nowhere. Much to my surprise, albeit reluctantly, my parents agreed the discipline would do me good and felt if I got out into the big wide world, it might get all that surplus energy – and the army – out of my system.

My hands have a will of their own, rebellious, unruly. Every time I yawn, they rise up in the air, and then flop down as I exhale onto my belly. Rebelling on my belly, fingers in defiant spasm. At least I can move my head a little– not off the pillow, it's still too heavy for that - but with superhuman effort, I can at least turn it from side to side.

Jeremy, a shaven-headed nurse in his 30s, is aware of my discomfort and stretches my fingers, splaying them out before placing my hands beside my hips.

"That should feel better now." He stares at me with reassurance.

"Tell you what, I'm going to fix you up with a buzzer so, if your hands start troubling you, or you need anything else, you can always call for help."

I reply by flicking my eyes upwards, letting Jeremy know that I've understood. True to his word, he attaches a buzzer to my pillow within reach of my head. "There! Now all you have to do is move your head to the side and the buzzer will ring. Think you can do that?" He watches as I try and, to my delight, I manage to move my head sufficiently to press the buzzer. It rings! At last I have the means to call for help, which I do several times in a day, buzzing for a nurse to come and put my hands in their rightful place, to itch my face, or to hold a bottle in place to pee, nope, too late!

So there we were, my parents and me, and suddenly the guy behind the desk passed me a sketch of a human body and asked me to mark it with what tattoos I had and where. Well, my Dad's face was a picture, as he'd no idea I'd been tattooed. He gazed wide-eyed at the tasteful headstone on my hip, green and yellow and shaped like a cross with an elegant 6 inch rose growing through it. The Recruiting Sergeant looked at me, smirking at the situation, at my Dad's disapproving frown. But that was me, always doing whatever I wanted, breaking all the rules I could.

Can't sleep for the beep! There's a mobile in reception which haunts me every night, blaring away incessantly as people ring to enquire about their children, parents, siblings, friends.....I drown it out by watching TV, comforting reruns of Walker, Texas Ranger or McGyver. That MacGyver - always getting into dangerous situations, always getting out of them with a clever device, a daring escape or a well-aimed fist. Wonder how he'd cope with MY situation?

So, some weeks later I was present and not-so-correct at the army selection trial in Chepstow. This began with a Basic Fitness Level test involving a series of radio beeps. We rookies had to run up and down a long hall in time to the beeps which got faster and faster while a PT officer kept his beady eye on us. How well (or not) you managed to keep up would determine the role you'd play in the military (or not). Really good runners qualified for the Paras but, although I was fairly fit, considering running wasn't my strongest point, I was assigned to the Infantry. In my defence, to qualify for infantry was a killer of a task for anyone – chin-ups, endless sit-ups and a few miles in a certain time - a massive day! I just scraped through that selection! JUST!

I couldn't wait for the first phase of my training to begin and started running straight away, weeks before my enlistment date, pounding through the streets of Wythenshawe where I lived at the time with my grandfather. Wythenshawe is a sprawling council estate – one of the biggest in Europe – and has quite a reputation for crime, yet I found the people warm and friendly and can honestly say some of the best days of my life were spent there. Possibly because my Grandad and other relatives spoilt me rotten and, within reason, I could pretty well do whatever I wanted.

That being said, the neighbourhood could be scary at night if you came across the wrong people and, logically or not, that's when I chose to train, thinking fear would push me harder as I went from lamppost to lamppost; running to one lamppost then sprinting to the next as my shadow crossed beneath the orange glow which shone back from smooth wet pavements. Determined to get myself fit, I'd even sacrificed my Ford Fiesta, swopping it with a mate for a pair of running shoes and sports kit. I also managed to settle the debts I'd run up with Gavin, drinking away his credit card, leaving me solvent, straight and literally footloose, so the adventure could begin.

Chapter 3

Hate the wheelchair. Sitting in it is agonising, putting pressure on my pathetically thin, bony backside. No help for it – just have to sit tight, unable to move, unable to complain, unable even to break wind. Literally a pain in the arse!

Wind is a particularly unpleasant by-product of locked-in; bad enough when you can let rip, but I can't; the air just stagnates in my gut, swelling my belly fit to burst. If anyone stuck a needle in me, I'd pop, blown to shreds like an overinflated balloon. Problem is the muscles don't work, so I can't push anything out, can't even empty my bowels unaided. Thank God for suppositories!

I was 19 years old and waiting at Royston Station with my fellow recruits. Eventually, the bus turned up and took us to ATR Bassingbourn where we'd be based for the next Ten weeks for Phase 1 training.

On arrival, we were greeted by a stern-looking NCO. "Drop your kit in the block and get outside pronto, you C.R.O.W.S!" he barked. (CROWS was a term used for any soldier in his first 3 years, I learned) COMBAT RECRUIT OF WAR!

Shortly afterwards, we rookies were standing on parade and the Sergeant was waiting for total silence, staring at us each in turn with the gravest expression. His opening statement was slow and ponderous, so as to add more weight to the occasion.

"YOU, my lads, are the luckiest recruits ever to come through those gates!" He explained that a bomb was found at Royston Station under one of the four buses, a welcoming gift no doubt from the IRA. Had it gone off while we were there, it could have killed up to 400 of us.

If I was unnerved by the experience, I didn't let it show. Instead I threw myself into my new routine with as much gusto as I could muster.

When my basic training finished, I was "passed off", a term used for being accepted as a soldier. I was glad – and quite relieved - to have survived this long and proud to be awarded the 'Best Rifle Shot medal' for using the LSW SA 80, a skill that's very hard to master - especially, as I did, without having SUSAT magnification eye and iron sights fixed on the weapon.

All my folks came along for my pass off, including my Grandad Derek. Proud as punch they were at this memorable occasion; which almost made those tortuous basic training treks worthwhile.

Everything's vague. Just the sensation of being rolled around the bed, side to side and back again as my sheets are changed. They need changing a lot as I've lost control of my bowels and keep shitting the bed. Must be those suppositories! All dignity gone, I pray to get it back, pray to stop fouling myself, pray just to be able to move again, to communicate and to let someone know how I'm feeling! Oh God, please help me!

The alarm bell goes off. It often goes off, every time someone's heart stops beating. Can hear nurses! "Code Blue!" "Code Blue!" and there's a mad rush of feet, patients dying, in need of reviving yet I'm still here, still alive. Please God, don't let me die, please God not yet.

Army life isn't all it's cracked up to be. To be perfectly frank, training for the Infantry is an experience I'd sooner forget, had it not had such a profound effect on me.

Think of the coldest, wettest place on earth, speed-marching at night for 30 kilometres at a stretch in damp clothes and sub-zero temperatures, sometimes as much as 10 degrees below, and you've some idea of the hell we faced in the raw, cold plains of the Brecon Beacons.

This was our training ground, a place so bleak that even hardened SAS men sometimes trained there. During one speed-march - also known as 'tabbing' – it started snowing, an absolute blizzard, cold enough to freeze my eyebrows solid, and I suffered a brain freeze while having a pee, falling over like a stiff board in the process. Thinking back to my practice runs around Manchester's suburbs made me smile at my own naivety. Ignorance is bliss!

Such expeditions were so traumatic that the officers had to con you into it. "Okay lads," they'd say, "we can stay here for another week or you can try and make it to the chopper 13km away." Naturally, we'd choose the chopper, knowing the RAF was conducting operations in the area. Anything was better than an extra week in the open with no creature comforts, not so much as a hot shower to look forward to at the end of the day. So off we'd Tab, desperate to get out of there, to reach the helicopter in time, on yet another blister-popping, foot-rotting, toe-bleeding stomp.

It was even worse when we stopped. Some recruits suffered hypothermia and I hated hearing them scream with the pain. Sometimes, they'd start hallucinating and have to be choppered home to barracks.

For the rest of us, we'd give anything for a smoke or a bar of chocolate. I once witnessed a Mars Bar being sold for twenty pounds, while a pack of cigarettes would easily go for fifty quid and even more.

My arms are still causing problems, ending up on top of my belly somehow, so nurses have to keep stretching them out and laying them tidily against my side, time and time again.

Now some bright spark has come up with these awful arm straighteners. Made of thick foam padding, they're fixed firmly onto my arms with their blue Velcro straps, making me feel hot, panicky and claustrophobic – as if I don't feel scared enough already! Every night at 8 o'clock, I pray another nurse will be on duty, yet sure enough it's her! I look into her eyes, pleading silently, trying to make her understand, to read my mind – no use!

In fact, she's smiling, no doubt believing she's doing the right thing.

"Your arms need to be kept straight," she explains. "Otherwise they could remain contorted, maybe for life."

With calm efficiency, she begins to imprison my reluctant limbs, while I shake my head frantically from side to side. Can't she see? She's ignoring my tears? Is she deliberately avoiding my imploring, desperate gaze?

Whether she realises how distressed I am or not, she continues with her task, trussing up my arms and tolerating no dissent from me. I feel like a mental patient in a straitjacket - not just due to the physical indignity, but because I have absolutely no say in the matter, no choice and no rights whatsoever.

Filled with rage, wracked with pain, and frustrated with powerlessness, I want to grab her hands to stop her and scream at the top of my voice: "Leave me ALONE! But of course she can't hear me. Dammit - no one can.

Oh please, God, I don't want to live like this! Please help me!

I was posted as part of a peace-keeping mission to Northern Ireland, a nice part of the world for all its problems. Our job was assisting the RUC who had a real struggle to control the streets, especially during the marching season. This used to scare the hell out of me, but then I was only 19. On some occasions, I found myself getting spat on, while at other times things got really hairy as angry protestors, up to 200 of them at once, faces scrunched with hatred, threw bricks and petrol bombs. All we squaddies could do was stand shoulder to shoulder, grasping our shields tightly and trying to hold the line while police did their best to calm the situation. When all else failed, and only as a last resort, we used baton guns, firing rubber bullets to disperse the crowd. It was an experience, shall we say.

Not everyone in Northern Ireland hated us. In time, I met a girl called Julie-Ann whose family were warm and hospitable. They would regularly invite me into their home for hot dinners and a taste of family life – something I'd been missing more than I'd expected.

Thanks to Julie-Ann, I was accepted by her friends and generally welcomed at the local pubs. I had to be careful, though, as there were clear Red Zones which British soldiers were strictly banned from entering. Many of the residents hated squaddies, and a wrong turning into their territory could literally result in death. In fact, the year before I arrived on the scene, twelve soldiers from my regiment were killed in a pub bombing – a man walked in, ordered a pint from the bar, drank up and calmly walked out again leaving a bag under the table. Moments later, it exploded, taking several lives in the process.

Jade squeezes my hand. She knows. She knows I'm here. "Is there anything you'd like to tell me?" I blink. I blink hard. I blink again. "Okay, I'm going to go through the alphabet and when I get to the right letter, just blink. Can you do that?" I blink. Then Jade starts saying the alphabet, slowly at first and when she gets to 'I', I blink. Finally, I can say what I've meaning to say all my life: "I-l-o-v-e y-o-u- J-a-d-e."

Much of my time in the army is a bit of a blur now, but certain incidents stand out, if only because they were terrifying. In my determination to escape the barracks every chance I could, I spent my first few month's wages on a car – a red Volkswagen Golf - which I loved. Having the freedom to go where I pleased when off duty helped make things more tolerable - until one Friday night. A group of NCOs approached, asking me to take them to a pub. Can't say I was thrilled at the prospect, as I'd planned to spend the evening at Julie-Ann's house. Her mother was cooking her famous Irish roast – the best I'd ever tasted. I never said 'No' to any of her food!

My first instinct was to refuse. Somebody or other was forever cadging lifts right, left and centre and I was fed up of being chauffeur. "Go on, Cogs, we'll give you thirty quid!" Well, thirty quid is thirty quid and, with Coleraine being just beyond Limavady where Julie-Ann lived, I agreed. "Okay then," I said, "but I'm leaving now."

Minutes later, three NCOs climbed into my Golf, all reeking of Lynx which, to this day, is a smell I just can't stomach. The overpowering mixture of Lynx with cheap aftershave was enough to make me gag, so how they thought they'd "pull" that night is anybody's guess. Still, hopes ran high.

"This pub's full of top totty, Cogs," said one of the guys. "Come in with us and check em out, you might score!" Tactfully, I declined, thinking of Julie-Ann's warm house and that mouth-watering Irish roast. Besides, except for Brophy - a huge, bald-headed guy with arms that bulged like Bluto's - I'd no time for them, as they'd made my life a misery from the first day I arrived at the battalion, sending me for fags and treating me like a slave (just C.R.O.W norm at the time!) It wasn't uncommon to be woken up in the middle of the night by drunken seniors wanting me to go on stupid errands for them, or just trying to intimidate me with bullying tactics, punching me in the head and leaving me too scared to sleep.

Humiliation was the order of the day. On one occasion, I was made to lie on the floor with my arms outstretched while two people sat on my arms, the idea being, supposedly, to see if you were strong enough to lift them. "Close your eyes and concentrate," rasped a senior private and when I did, he parked his naked bottom on my face, rubbing my nose in it, while his cronies laughed their sides sore.

Fortunately, since writing this chapter, the British army have clamped down on bullying, which is good news for new recruits. Congratulations to the military for taking action against all forms of abuse.

Can't move. Arms like lead. Helpless, hopeless, humiliated.

Another time, I was dragged into a room full of older serving soldiers – about 20 of them – stripped, made to stand on a Dobey Bin in the middle of the room and forced to answer vile, disgusting questions about my mother and girlfriend. Fortunately, the Sergeant interrupted their sick game before things went any further, but this episode was typical of the treatment meted out to raw, young recruits. Whether it was to break our spirit or to toughen us up, I'll never know. Don't want to either.

Now here they were again, sitting not-so-pretty in my pride and joy, no doubt thinking they'd done me a favour by including me in on their next stupid jaunt. But Brophy was cool.

"Pick us up at one o'clock sharp, all right, Cogs?" Brophy said, unwinding his considerable bulk from the front seat. I sighed with relief as my remaining passengers disembarked and headed up the steps to the pub's main entrance.

It was a large, okay looking pub in the centre of Coleraine but what nobody had told me was that it also lay in the middle of a red zone, a definite no-go for squaddies! Blissfully ignorant of the events to come, I set off for Julie-Ann's, with my newly acquired sound system at full blast. At last I was free. In my own private space with my own choice of music thud-thudding, I felt like the bees-knees as I turned into the estate where Julie-Ann lived with her family and parked up near their modest terraced house. The smell of the roast was divine. After a week of exhausting patrols, I was ready for a good meal in excellent company, then chilling on the sofa with a DVD. Julie-Ann's parents and brother were exceptionally kind and friendly, always laughing (the 'crack' was the term), always making me feel wanted. Here I could relax and be treated as a human being for a change.

All too soon, the dreaded deadline approached, and I uncurled myself reluctantly from all these creature comforts. To be honest, I almost didn't go. Part of me felt justified in leaving the men to walk it back to barracks, but then conscience got the better of me. Besides, I liked Brophy and didn't want to see him stuck. Brophy had never abused me.

Back at the pub, it was half an hour before the more respectable patrons started trickling out, and by this time I was tired, fed up and just wanted to get back to barracks. Turning my headlights on so the guys would know I was waiting, I saw Brophy's bald head glowing orange under the street lights as he and the others stepped out into the street. Impatiently, I flashed my lights again, but they were just hanging round, no doubt hoping for a last-minute cop off. "So the Lynx didn't work then," I thought to myself with a smile of satisfaction.

Suddenly, one of the Irish blokes started arguing with Brophy....apparently it was over some comment Brophy made to the man's wife, not realising she was already spoken for. I don't think they came to an agreement, because suddenly the Irish bloke, obviously fuelled with Guinness and chasers, smashed a bottle over Brophy's head.

All hell broke loose; Brophy pulled the guy to the ground and started fisting him in the face, and within seconds, everything went crazy with everyone throwing punches. By now the whole pub had emerged, at least 40 of them, all with their dander up, screaming blue murder and joining in the fray. Brophy and Co were hopelessly outnumbered and I briefly wondered whether I ought to wade in and help, but common sense prevailed. After all, if I got killed, who'd drive the guys home?

So I sat and watched with my heart racing, not sure of why it was happening. Brophy was still hitting the instigator, while some other bloke was hanging from his neck, trying to strangle him. I must say, Brophy put up a tremendous fight, elbowing his unwanted passenger while exchanging punches with the first guy. Bruce Lee wasn't in it! But then the first man smashed another bottle over him.

Realising the battle was lost, Brophy and his two companions ran for my car, with half of Northern Ireland in hot pursuit. Desperate and shaking with fear, I wound down the window on the passenger side to give them a better chance of escape and, with 40 angry Irishmen hot on their heels, they clambered in.

"Drive, Cogs! Drive!" they yelled. I didn't need telling twice and had already got my foot on the accelerator. The drink-crazed crowd tried to block our escape but I simply gritted my teeth and drove straight through them at a great rate of knots.

"Squaddie bastards!" A hail of bottles hit my car, smashing the windows and hands reached in to grab us. One man got me by the sleeve of my hoodie, and all four occupants braced ourselves, trying to stop the mob from dragging us out of the vehicle, knowing we'd be killed for sure. For several moments, it was touch and go, with men climbing over my roof and bonnet, until at last the man who'd grabbed my arm let go. I revved furiously and the car leapt forward, gathering speed and sending the unwanted hitchers flying. Satisfied I'd put enough distance between the car and our pursuers, I glanced in the mirror.

Never in my life have I seen such hatred in human faces as I did just then. Refusing to give up, the mob kept chasing us and, as I wheelspun out of the car park, I thanked God I'd been practicing getaway driving that week.

Showered in glass, covered in blood, the other soldiers started laughing with adrenalin and intense relief. "Well done, Coggers!" they yelled and slapped me on the back. For the first time, they treated me with respect and, in spite of my fears, I felt elated. I'd been part of something.

Once back at the barracks, however, my spirits sank. The car was a total write-off and, even though the guys were making out I was a hero, all I really cared about was how I'd get it fixed and who was going to pay for it. The next morning, I received £140 for £3,000 of damage. I was gob-smacked.

That little episode opened my eyes. All the adventures and derring-do heroics I'd expected from the army disappeared overnight. I realised some blokes would never be my brothers-in-arms or ever take a bullet for me and I decided to leave as soon as my 3 years were up. That said, great mates WERE forged without a doubt! But little did I know I'd be leaving sooner than I thought.

Hot, so hot, sweating like mad. I blink while Jade says the alphabet again. "P-i-l-l-o-w--o-f-f". Relief as she removes the pillow, letting me breathe again, free from the sweltering heat.

Mum's here now, trying to lift my arms over Jade to give her a hug, but they're dead weights and I scream out crying, can't even hold them round her neck. Mum tries again when I'm put on my side so my arms stay in place due to gravity, but it's not the same. I can't feel anything and I so badly want to hold her, and I cry. Jade lies with me, both of us crying and me panicking, thinking I'll never be able to squeeze her again and never be able to talk to her. It's devastating. I'm in bits.

Oh no, I need a pee! Too late, I've no control, it's already on its way and I can't stop it, so I'm peeing all over her, peeing all over Jade. She jumps up with shock and her jeans are soaked and I just keep peeing, peeing the bed. Amazing how a few hours in one's own urine helps one see life differently.

Have just been fitted with a catheter bag. A couple of nurses brought a trolley full of tools and placed a' bluey' over me, a piece of blue crepe paper with a hole in the middle for my penis to fit through. Then they held up this plastic rod with a small ball on the end and a plastic hose to feed to urine into the bag. After applying some jelly, one nurse began to slide the rod into my urethra. Ouch! It stung all the way down. I still haven't got used to the pain, but at least I'm starting to think more clearly. And I'm a lot drier.

Chapter 4

Although I hated most of my time in the army, I did find some good mates, one of whom, Damien, changed my life forever. Damien came from Stockport, not far from where I was living at the time, so it was only natural that, with both of us on leave for a month, we should journey there together.

After a short ferry crossing, I drove him home, unaware how my life was about to change. Standing by the gate was a stunning girl with a baby on her hip. Now, hard as it may be for some people to believe, and it's something I'd never have thought possible until that moment, it really was love at first sight. This was The One.

"That's my sister," said Damien, following my gaze, and as we approached, the girl's face lit up with the most incredible smile I'd ever seen.

"Hi, kiddo!" said Damien and he leapt out of the passenger seat to embrace his sibling. Eventually, they broke off hugging each other long enough for introductions. The girl gazed at me, a puzzled look in her gorgeous blue eyes. "Hello," she said. "Oh – this is my mate, Pete. Pete, meet my sister Jade."

In a matter of seconds, I was head over heels in love. Staying at Damien's that weekend, I got to know Jade more than many people I'd known for a lifetime and it soon became obvious she felt the same about me. Nothing happened between us – she was just 15 at the time - but we promised to write, a correspondence we kept up for several months, writing every day, her letters driving me crazy with the scent of her Tommy Girl perfume.

We'd talk about anything and everything, page after page after page, so I found myself writing instead of going to the NAAFI. No wonder I never became one of the 'in crew'. But I didn't care. All I wanted was to do my job and get back to my room to write to Jade – until her mother put a stop to it, threatening to report me to my commanding officer who'd have put me in jail for sure. Not that I blamed her, of course – Jade was legally speaking under-age and besides, her brother was my fellow soldier and a good friend. But it was difficult. How was I not to write to her when she wanted to keep writing to me? For both of us, it was a forbidden love, and we couldn't do a damn thing about it. For months afterwards, life sucked.

Who'd have thought a simple board with letters on it could mean so much. Thanks to the alphabet board, I can 'talk' to nurses, spelling out any problems, such as the one I have with my hands, by blinking. I'm also using it to convey my thoughts and feelings, using different members of staff to write them in a book, along with details of everything that happens to me.

What a lifeline! Now, when Jade, Mum, Dad and other visitors arrive, all they have to do is read my book to know what's going on. At the moment, it's full of arguments with various medicos, mainly over sleeping pills. I'm on 2 tablets every 4 hours to try and knock me out, as I spend most of the night trying to move my fingers – every minute, in fact. I'm so desperate to start moving again!

While on Army operations, writing letters was about the only thing to do. (Nowadays, I expect most are on email, but all we got in the 90s were free envelopes.) About the most exciting thing we did was an attempted robbery, carefully planned after running out of fags. We were billeted at a police station in Strabane at the time, helping out the RUC and for some reason our pay hadn't come through.

"Guess what?" said my mate Andy, "Just heard you can get free fags from the machine in the police canteen." Say no more; me and Andy made straight for the canteen ready to put this rumour to the test.

The canteen was now closed, with just dim lights from the corridor and the cigarette machine, which stood in all its tantalising glory by the wall. I tried tugging one of the drawers. "You've got to turn it upside down first," said Andy. "You keep a look out while I give it some wellie!"

Next thing, Andy's ragged the machine upside down and managed to extract over ten packets, so off we went, puffing away, chuffed to have got away with our crime.

Only we hadn't. Days later, we were arrested, instantly recognised from the CCTV! Well, how were we to know a cop shop would have security cameras? Fingerprints, mug shots, the lot, but at least we had a choice as to how we'd be charged, either as civilians or by the army in which case we wouldn't have a record. Naturally, I chose the latter, knowing full well my Dad would have kittens if he ever found out! As it was, the punishment was bad enough – a month being marched around camp, chance parades and brushing the floor of an aircraft hangar till our hands bled. It was worth it, though, not to disappoint my Dad.

Night is horrible. Lying here, scared. Don't know if I'll make it. Same as last night, the night before and the night before... too many nights. Someone's cut a hole in my neck and there's no way to breathe except through a pipe stuck in my neck and suddenly I'm suffocating 'cos the pipe's blocked again and no one's around. Not for the first time, I appeal to the only person who can get me through this. Please God help me!

Hate the nights; long, silent deathly nights when I don't know whether I'll survive until the dawn. You'd think when you can't move that nothing could happen – but that's not true. When you can't move, anything could happen. My trachea gets blocked so I can't breathe.

And then there's the hands; my hands. I can't move them! I've no control over them or, for that matter, over any part of what's left of my body. But my arms have a life of their own, moving separately with no input from me whatsoever. Every time I yawn, I can only watch helplessly as my hands rise of their own accord and I can't flex my triceps or do anything to stop them. These hands, these aliens, keep moving upwards, blocking the hole in my neck - they're literally trying to suffocate me! And in my head I'm screaming, "Please God help me!"

He must be listening, he must be hearing, as somehow I make it through and then I'm cursing the dawn 'cos I'm still alive. Wish Jade was here!

I never forgot Jade completely, but life moved on, my depression lifted and some months later I met Julie-Ann who was to be part of my life for the next four years. She was an awesome laugh, and great to be around, making me feel very loved and I felt she was sent to me for sure during my time in Northern Ireland. Both of us talked of settling down in the UK and when I got transferred to a garrison in Chepstow, South Wales, it seemed only natural for Julie-Ann to come with me. And that's where I faced the first massive blow of my life.

Just been for a scan. As Geoff, my nurse, wheels me back into my room, I see a small Asian woman dressed entirely in black with a large cross around her neck. Initially, I'm disturbed by her nun-like appearance; has she come to pray over me, give me the Last Rites? She waits quietly, smiling as Geoff settles me in and makes sure I'm comfortable. I gaze back at her, transfixed. After Geoff has gone, she approaches the bed and introduces herself.

"Hello. My name is Eva. I've been asked to visit you from time to time, to see if I can help in any way." She glances down at my alphabet board. "Is this your board? Can I give it a try, see how it works?"

Gently, Eva takes the board and we start a brief conversation, Eva reading out the letters, me blinking. It's hesitant at first, but by the time Eva leaves, she's mastered the board and I've made a valuable new friend.

Julie-Ann and I had just set up home and were settling in nicely when the 'lump' appeared. The size of a golf ball, it arrived on my neck literally overnight. For some weeks beforehand, I'd been suffering from a nasty, persistent cough that slowed me down on platoon runs, much to the disgust of my Sergeant who kept pushing me harder and harder until I couldn't catch my breath. The Medical Officer thought it was asthma and put me on inhalers but they didn't do any good and I got cheesed off with the Sergeant yelling at me to "pull my f***ing feet up!" and hitting me with his Kevlar helmet.

Then we saw the lump. In fact, everyone saw it. "What's that on your neck, son?" asked my Dad during a lad's lunch out, and suddenly my beer and Carbonara lost their flavour, as I realised the lump could no longer be ignored.

Even so, I was determined to carry on as usual. After going for an X-ray one Monday morning, I re-joined my unit for dry mortar drills on the field but hadn't been there long when a Land Rover pulled up on the grass behind me. It was my mate Buggie. "Get in Pete," he said. "Your locker's packed and you're going to hospital." What a thing to hear so soon after an X-ray. I was pretty scared to say the least.

Four hours later at Frimley Park Hospital, I was being tested with CT scans, followed by a bronchoscopy, a horrible ordeal. I should have known something bad was going to happen when two nurses each grabbed one of my hands, saying "It'll be over in a minute, you'll be okay." Next news, someone shoves a camera down my throat and I feel I'm going to choke.

It was Hodgkin's Lymphoma – cancer of the lymph glands. Surely there was some mistake; I was so young and wanted to do so much with my life. What a 21st birthday *this* turned out to be!

Eva is an absolute gem! She sits by my bed and reads some of my jottings, crying at some, laughing at others – it's such a relief to have someone share my thoughts, to understand the pain and fear and fury going on in this

41

wretched, useless body, shouting out from the tortured
recess of my mind.

The specialist put me on a course of chemotherapy straight away, with radio therapy later on. My dad was living in Anglesey, North Wales at the time, so I decided to move there and have treatment at Bangor hospital – not just for the parental support but - vital for a young lad - so nobody I knew would see me when I lost my hair – nobody except for Julie-Ann, of course, who came with me.

Hundreds of pills and steroids did their trick, but caused my crowning glory to fall out fairly quickly. Perhaps as well, seeing as I knew it was going to happen anyway. I was watching TV at the time. I just stroked my head and saw great clumps of hair hit the sofa. So as not to scare Julie-Ann, I got up quietly, went into the bathroom and locked myself in. "Well," I thought to myself, "if it's going to come out anyway, it may as well be all at once," and I started shaving my head, saying goodbye to the way I looked and trying not to cry. I had to stay strong; I was going to beat this thing and that's all I could tell myself, the only way I could think.

As part of my treatment, surgeons carved a lymph node out of my neck, and I woke up from the operation feeling dazed and desperate for a leak. From my hospital bed I could see the toilet just across the corridor, just ten steps away, so I climbed out of the bed and tried to make my own way there.

Weak and groggy, I'd only managed a couple of paces when I started swaying in the corridor, as weak and faint as a Jane Austen heroine, wearing this ridiculous gown with my lily-white bottom exposed. Suddenly, I lost my balance completely and hit the deck like a sack of manure. "What's happened to me?" I thought, "I'm 21 years old and can't even walk to the loo!"

As I lay on the cold, polished floor, I noticed a stream of crimson and realised a drainage bag attached to my neck had been yanked away by my exertions, ripping the stitches in my neck. Blood splattered everywhere and my neck was dripping plasma while I remained on the floor, scared and helpless. Fortunately, a nurse saw me lying there with my bum hanging out and ran towards me shouting for help. I felt like a dying dog, unable even to lift my head.

Worse was to come. As the treatment progressed, my joints hurt more and my wrists and knees stiffened, making stairs harder to climb. I hated what was happening to me. I felt like a pensioner, a bald-headed, stiff-kneed, creaky-jointed old man.

Slowly but surely, I began to get better and, one year later, I thanked God for Dr Node and his magic milkshake of chemo. Julie-Ann, my Dad and the rest of my family all helped me through the dark times, with Mum visiting as often as she could, seeing as she'd separated from my Dad and was still living up in Derbyshire.

Once given the 'all clear', feeling fit and with a full head of hair again, I headed back to Manchester to find work. Due to my illness, the army had released me so I went back to bricklaying, this being the only trade I knew, and found a job with a great guy called Simon Hood who taught me all he knew – more than I ever learned at college – starting me off on a lucrative building career. Working for him was fun too.

People keep trying to tell me something, about what's wrong with me, about how I'm quadriplegic or whatever the word is, and even my Mum who nurses quadriplegics believes it, but I can't take it in. Or maybe I just don't want to - in denial. Not me!

Every day, there are hushed voices which I can't quite catch, saying things like how I "must be brave," "mustn't expect too much," "got to face up to things." Me thinking, "Be brave." Yeah right! How can I face up to this?" Once, I thought I could hear Jade talking to a doctor, telling him not to keep harping on about it in front of me, begging him to say he simply doesn't know, which, let's face it, is only the truth. Nobody knows what someone else is capable of. Nobody. Besides, Jade won't let me give up; she keeps pumping me with inspirational stories she's found on the internet, refusing to believe I won't get better, refusing to let me stop trying.

So now the mutterings are kept outside in the corridor, with people saying, "don't tell him." But then I could be imagining it. I imagine all sorts of things lying here.

The cancer had taken its toll on me mentally as well as physically, so I did what most young males would do to dull the memories – took to the bottle. One night, after a particularly heavy drinking session, Julie-Ann and I had a massive fight, one that had been brewing over months of emotional turmoil. Looking back, I now had a different outlook on life and what I wanted. Julie-Ann and I had grown apart, so much so. I'd become more focused on work and harder to live with. Well, no one's that easy going after a bottle of Scotch. After downing the lot, I completely lost it and ended up putting my fist through an opaque glass window and ripping my hand to shreds. I was a bit hot headed like that.

Needless to say, it wasn't long before we split up and Julie-Ann went back to Northern Ireland - not that I blamed her. Of course, I felt guilty, but everything had changed. So regretfully, Julie-Ann, and I said "goodbye". It was a sad parting for me, as I really cared about her a lot. We'd had some great times together and I'll always love her for supporting me during my chemo. She was truly an angel. But I had a different future now.

I'm laughing, can't help it; uncontrollable bursts of weird, inhuman gurgles emerging from both ends of me. One of laughter, one of shit. This happens every night, mouth laughing, bowels emptying, having my bum wiped clean like a new-born baby, unable to apologise for the

steaming, rancid, foul-smelling mess. All I can do is breathe
out this strange hysterical laughter, as if I'm in shock, as if
my brain is somehow tricking me into feelings of hilarity;
while inside, I'm crying with shame.

Elsewhere in the hospital, someone is begging for ice-
cream, pressing the buzzer over and over again, then
screaming, screaming all night long like a banshee in a
horror movie. Then I hear a man saying, "Hello, Nurse!
Hello Nurse! Hello! Nurse!" until I think I'm in a crazy
home.

"Hello, Pete. It's me, Jade." At the sound of her sweet
voice, I nearly dropped the pint of ale I was holding. My
chemo now a mercifully fading memory, I was back at
work, doing well and enjoying a regular drink with my
mates at home when the phone rang. Damien's beautiful
sister had remembered me. "How are you?" she asked.
What I *wanted* to say was, "My heart's pounding, my legs
have gone to jelly and if happiness was a disease I'd gladly
die of it here and now!" What I actually said was far less
dramatic but no doubt conveyed my surprised delight to
hear from her again. "I wondered if I could come over
sometime," she said. I was over the moon - Jade, the love
of my life not only remembered me but wanted to see me
again. So obviously I said "Yes."

Chapter 5

Back to the night screams in the corridor, phone going all the time keeping me awake. I need to be asleep. I need those hours of precious oblivion from this unrelenting horror, from my own twisted, useless body. A new nurse comes in, a big lady with big afro hair and I want her to bring me some earplugs to drown out the noise. Regular staff know now that when I lift my eyes repeatedly it means to get my alpha-board please, but this lady's no regular. I've never seen her before. She obviously hasn't the foggiest what I'm trying to say, even though I'm staring at the board which is lying on the table, willing her to guess, but all she does is lean over me. "What –Do – You- Want?" she shouts as if I'm deaf. I just look at her, thinking "Is she for real?" like I'm going to say, "Yeah, thanks, I'll have a Big Mac 'n' fries please!"

Finally, she reaches for the alphabet board and then things get really stupid. She picks up my lifeless hand and points it at the board, moving my forefinger across the letter: 'T-o-i-l-e-t'. Does she really think she knows what I want? I just stare at her in disbelief and, by shifting my head to one side (the only part that of me that moves) try to press the buzzer that's safety-pinned to my pillow.

She stares at me with little comprehension, shaking her head as my face contorts with frustration and my eyes flick frantically up and down. Finally, she reaches a decision. "No, NO!" I scream inside, "Not that, please not that!" But it's no use.

Slowly and deliberately, she reaches down and removes my buzzer.

Jade and I fell in love again, as deeply and wholeheartedly as before, only this time she was older and her mum wouldn't stand in our way. Who could? There was no courtship as such – we were so obsessed with each other, we just moved in together straightaway, renting a place in Chapel-en-le-Frith on the border of

Derbyshire High Peak. There was no real plan and hardly any furniture. We didn't care. All we wanted was to be together.

Thanks to my regular nurses, I've now got my buzzer back, thank God - that and the alphabet board are my lifelines!

Mum's here, her presence comforting, her voice calm and reassuring, as if I were five years old again and frightened of the bogey man. Only this is no fantasy – this monster is real. Earlier, I heard her talking to the doctor who said I needed a peg feed fitted to my stomach and it's scared the hell out of me! My eyelids start twitching and Mum reaches for the alphabet board, holding it up and tracing the letters with her forefinger as I spell out my message. "P-l-e-a-s-e h-e-l-p m-e. C-a-n-'t g-o o-n l-i-k-e t-h-i-s. P-l-e-a-s-e, M-u-m, h-e-l-p m-e t-o d-i-e."

"You don't mean that!" Mum bites her lip, her face pale and crumpled as she forces back the tears. She shakes her head, but I'm unrelenting, my eyes flicking frantically up and down to get my message across. "I d-o m-e-a-n i-t. I w-a-n-t t-o d-i-e. Y-o-u a-r-e a n-u-r-s-e. H-e-l-p m-e." She turns away so I know she's crying now and doesn't want me to see. Why is everyone so determined not to cry? Have they all vowed to be cheerful all the time, like holiday camp redcoats? She turns back now, takes a long, deep breath and takes my hand in hers.

"Look Peter!" she sighs. "I know how you must be feeling..."

"No, you don't! You don't!" I'm screaming inside, but she can't hear me.

"...and I understand, really I do...."

Her voice trails off. She can see my eyes burning. All of a sudden, she shakes off the veil of helplessness she's been carrying and I recognise my Mum from 20 years ago - the kind, no-nonsense woman who'd tuck me up in bed at night, loving and efficient, calming me to sleep. "Give it 3 months.

Another 3 months. And if you're no better....well, then we'll discuss it. Okay? Okay Peter?"

Using the alphabet board, I spelled out one last word: "P-r-o-m-i-s-e."

Mum paused, chewing her lip again, then nodded in agreement and squeezed my hand. "I promise."

Life with Jade was awesome. That first year together was the happiest we'd ever known. Even though the English weather got me down a bit at times (laying bricks in the middle of a deluge or a Force 9 gale in Derbyshire wasn't much fun), having Jade to come home to at the end of the day was all I really needed to keep me smiling.

If it wasn't for my mum, we'd probably still be in Chapel-en-le-Frith!

Mum took a trip to Australia, visiting family in the hills of Mount Helena near Perth. They were always telling me to come over, insisting "the Aussie life would suit you here," and "You should give it a try." Well, after cold winters and chapped hands, the thought of wall-to-wall sunshine down under grew more and more appealing so, one day after Jade had finished work at Top Shop, I asked what she thought of the idea. Her answer came as a shock. "Okay," she said, just like that.

We then applied for a work visa and started saving like mad for our trip. Once the decision had been made, scraping the snow off the bricks every morning was a little more tolerable.

In fact, life couldn't be more exciting. We were in love and we were about to start our new life on the other side of the world – what could possibly go wrong?

Robin, my speech therapist, has just fixed a speaking valve over my trachea to see if I can talk with it. I try to say something, breathing as hard as I can, but all I get is a loud whizzing sound, a bit like those air fresheners people use in cars with plastic propellers. It scares the hell out of me!

To make things worse, Jade's sister Amber arrives for a visit, having just flown in from England, boyfriend Chris in tow. Can't say I've made a great impression, wheezing through this dratted valve! I should be glad to see them, I know, but I feel so humiliated at their having to look at me in this miserable state.

All I want to do is hold Amber in my arms, ask how she is and tell her how pleased I am to see her, but I can't say anything. All I can do is lie here, wheezing through this stupid valve and howling with tears, as I realise (for the first time) that she is here to visit her sister in Perth, it's not to have a good time; there'll be no sailing down the river on my boat, or running along the beach, or even throwing a shrimp on a barbie. Instead, she's here to comfort Jade who's on the verge of a nervous breakdown due to weeks of staring at a mere husk of the man I used to be – a head moving side to side on a lifeless body.

Jade is missing me terribly, missing me next to her as we drift off to sleep at night. Now all she has is an old T-shirt of mine which she holds against her face, trying to recapture the mixed smell of my body and aftershave. As for me, the pain of this enforced separation is killing me while the thought of never spooning my warm, beautiful woman is unbearable. An artist friend has painted Jade's portrait for me to gaze at, which motivates me to keep going, to never give up, until me and Jade can be together again.

Perth, Western Australia is a glorious place. Mum met us at the airport and, as she drove us down to Hillary's Boat Harbour, we gasped with amazement at its sheer beauty.

Just a few months later, we realised this was where we wanted to be. There was plenty of work for bricklayers, I was earning good money and the sun was always shining. Applying for permanent residency was an absolute no-brainer....

It must be over a month now – or is it two? Three? Time's meaningless anyway, just lying here hour after hour, day after day with no purpose, only waiting, desperate for release.

She promised....

To help keep my spirits up, Jade's been telling me about other recovering locked-in survivors she found online, who used all kinds of psychological tricks, such as visualisation, to help get different parts of the body moving again.

Inspired by their experiences, I lie awake at night, imagining I'm a crab with hands like pincers, willing my fingers to close together – two fingers and a thumb, just as a crab or lobster claw does. Mentally, I visualise them, beg them and pray for them to move - night after night after night, so many nights I can't even count.

And now the nights have turned into weeks, and I've woken up again to yet another day and I'm just staring upwards, watching streaks of sunlight playing upon the ceiling. How I yearn to feel the natural warmth of day instead of this cloying heat, this sticky prison of a hospital bed. And then I notice my thumb.

It moved! Only about two millimetres, but it definitely moved! Maybe I'm seeing things; maybe my wild imaginings have taken over! Frowning with concentration, I fix my eyes on the thumb, again willing it to life and am rewarded by a twitch – very faint, but a definite twitch!

I burst into deep, gut-busting sobs and ring my buzzer. Immediately, footsteps can be heard, someone running up the corridor and my nurse Cora comes in, thinking there's an emergency yet wondering why I'm smiling. Crying and smiling at the same time. She picks up the alphabet board and I start to blink: "L-o-o-k a-t m-y t-h-u-m-b," and she does, and now she's smiling too.

"Good on you, Pete! I knew you could do it!" she says and then I start blinking again, not easy through the tears. "P-l-e-a-s-e p-h-o-n-e J-a-d-e."

Initial homesickness aside, both Jade and I soon settled in Perth, an idyllic place for young couples wanting to build a future. There was just one problem. In order to stay in Perth, I had to find a sponsor, someone who could guarantee my wages for the first 2 years.

Help came from an unexpected source, a local builder called Joe who owned a large company in the city, and was prepared to take me on. Thanks to him, I learned how to make aluminium window frames and found a great friend in Bob Haynes, the guy who taught me; a genial man who smoked not so much like a chimney as a Titanic-sized funnel, Bob was cool, laid-back and an absolute ringer for John Wayne.

Everything was perfect – well, almost. Every so often, we had to leave the country for me to renew my visa, which was disconcerting to say the least. Each journey cost us a couple of grand, left us jet-lagged for a week and made us wonder whether we were coming or going. Complicating things even further, 3 years into my job, there was a pay dispute between the company and some Filipino workers, resulting in us all losing our sponsorship rights. We were sent a letter, giving us 28 days to leave the country! Our only option was to go to my father's home in Thailand where we stayed for several months, existing in a state of limbo. Until, in what seemed likely to be our final trip to Perth, we returned on a holiday visa to collect the rest of our things and spent a feverish few days phoning and emailing in a desperate last ditch attempt to find another sponsor before being ruthlessly banished from the Land of Oz.

Hundreds of telephone calls later, and after much begging and pleading, I was about to give up. It looked as though our dream was over and we were destined to return to the bleak grey mists of Blighty.

"Just try once more," said Jade, putting a comforting hand on my shoulder. I felt like J R Hartley in the Yellow Pages ad! With a sigh, I tapped in the next number on the list. It was a local guy, a builder called Jason Cherry.

"Ok," he said, "I'll give you a try." And in that moment, our worries were over.

I'm so excited, can't wait to show Jade – just to let her know that things are happening, that she shouldn't give up on me, so that she'll please, please wait for me! Vicky and her husband Brad are already here but, although I'm glad they've come, I hardly spare them a glance. I'm too transfixed by my resurrected thumb. Vicky follows my gaze and smiles at me, knowing it's the start of things to come.

Jade arrives, her face wreathed in smiles. She bends over to kiss me, asks me how I am and then looks at my thumb, which is still wiggling like an earthworm after a rainstorm.

"You're amazing!" says Jade. "Just amazing!"

The good news spreads like wildfire. Before long, everyone knows about my progress. On her weekly round, my regular doctor, Dr Steel is accompanied by a consultant - Neurologist and Stroke Physician Professor David Blacker who, after carefully examining my toes and thumb, looks me in the face. I stare back at him, mentally begging him to say the words I'm desperate to hear. "You're going to get well."

His actual words aren't quite so positive. "Well, Pete, you've a long road ahead of you, I'm sure you realise that?" I blink my eyes as meaningfully as I can. "It may seem a hard one too, so don't get discouraged if things take longer than you'd like. In fact, you'll probably need anti-depressants for the indefinite future – a good few years at least." He turns to my usual doctor, who nods in agreement. Then Professor Blacker makes the decision that could transform my life.

"I'd like to get him over to Shenton Park for rehabilitation."

Rehabilitation! This is something that I later learn is rarely, if ever, prescribed for a locked-in patient as badly affected as I am. Which can only mean one thing - there IS hope! In one short sentence, Professor Blacker has handed me a future, and I try to help the process along by imagining thousands of volts being zapped throughout my body, regenerating its neural pathways in readiness. Can't wait to begin, but it could be a while before a spare bed comes available, maybe in a couple of weeks.

Meanwhile, my physio Leanne has arranged for one of her old patients to visit me. Although he suffered a different condition to me and was in ICU a lot longer than I was, Ronan has learned to move and talk at Shenton Park. One year on and he's doing really well. Just listening to someone in the same boat is highly encouraging and I'm looking forward to more visits from my new friend....and whether it's due to Professor Blacker or Ronan, my other thumb has now begun to twitch. So have my knees!

Chapter 6

Everything's clearer now. I'm beginning to make sense of things, about how I came to be here, what's happened to me and what lies ahead in the future. The future! Just a couple of weeks ago I didn't HAVE a future, but now....

I can move! I can actually move. Okay, it's only my thumb and knees and then only by a flick of a switch you'd miss if you blinked, but if I can move ANY part of my body, even the smallest most insignificant part, then surely one day I can move the Earth!

Apparently, soon after I was admitted, the doctors told Jade and the family in no uncertain terms that any improvement in my condition would have to be sooner rather than later. No wonder she was so excited and relieved. It seems the pathways in my body are beginning to reconnect with my visions and concentration – I dare to believe.

Now that I can think more logically, I've managed to glean a few details about my illness. Locked-In Syndrome (LIS for short), sometimes known as 'disease of the walled living', is a neurological condition that's difficult to diagnose because patients don't respond to stimuli. As a result, they're often assumed to be comatose or in a vegetative state. Main causes are brain haemorrhage or injury, damage to the pons area of the brain, diseases that destroy the myelin sheath which protects nerve cells, and a massive brain stem stroke which is what happened to me.

Whatever the cause, the effects are devastating. Although unable to move, sufferers retain their cognitive and intellectual powers but can only communicate through vertical eye movements - the only voluntary muscles still functioning. Even this ability may go undetected for some time, as was the case with me, and it's usually spotted, not by scans or medical intervention, but by regular carers or close family and friends.

LIS is mercifully rare. Unfortunately, there's no known cure or treatment to date, the only help available being assistive technology to improve communication.

I'll never know whether it's down to my crab claw visualisation, but I've now discerned some movement in my left toes too, something I hadn't willed or even expected – they just started twitching while a nurse was putting my socks on.

So now the nights, the long sleepless nights are almost bearable. Now, when I lie awake, I'm no longer crushed by haunting fears and nightmares. I no longer fear the shadows or feel hollow with despair. Now, I'm focused on getting well. On getting OUT OF HERE!

The job, as a full-time bricklayer, brought in reasonable money, enough for us to pay our bills and plan for the future. But then human plans can never be guaranteed, no matter how hard we try to fulfil them. Bright as things seemed to be, neither Jade nor I could have planned for the storms which were about to affect our lives.

As the brain fog starts to clear, I'm coming to terms with this strange half-life in which even ordinary objects take on immense significance. Once, I thought nothing could matter more to me than my Volkswagen Golf. Now it all boils down to a simple board with letters on.

As my only means of communication, the alphabet board is my most essential piece of kit. The only problem is that it involves two people – me and whoever is trying to decode my blinks. Some of the nurses, like Cora, are brilliant, but some haven't the foggiest how the alphabet board works, which gets pretty frustrating. When I get out of here, I'll be pushing for all nurses to be trained and tested in its use, so no one else in my position has to be constantly misunderstood.

My board has all the letters of the alphabet spread four to a line down the board. Each line is a different

colour – yellow, red, blue, pink, grey, orange and green.
After making sure both they and I can see the board and
starting from the top, the person holding it calls out each of
the colours in turn until I blink, raising my eyes repeatedly,
so they know the letter I want is on that particular line.
Then they call the letters one by one, again waiting for me
to raise my eyes for the relevant one. This process takes
ages, but the nurses are usually pleased, as I generally spell
out a compliment. I may not be able to walk or talk, but
even in this condition, I can still chat up the girls!

Besides, I find these pleasantries pay dividends; if I
say something nice to someone; they're more willing to use
the board again, even though most of my messages tend to
involve embarrassing bodily functions. Two young nurses
got very confused recently when I spelt out the word "s-h-i-
t" – not just once but several times until finally, I added the
words "I h-a-v-e." Still they didn't cotton on, so I kept on
spelling, "s-h-i-t I h-a-v-e," until a certain odour began to
hit the air. At last, truth dawned and we all started
laughing. Before long, I was clean and dry again. Good job
nurses have a sense of humour!

That first storm was quite something. Unbelievably
dramatic. A cyclone from up north brought 150km winds
ripping across the coast, bringing down trees, smashing
cars and twisting everything in its path. Helpless in the
face of its incredible power, all anyone could do was to sit
tight and wait for the havoc to pass over.

Most people were affected, including me and Jade.
An incredible whiplash destroyed our fence and, petrified
by the storm, my dog Cody ran out into the road, straight
under the wheels of a car. What made the situation even
worse was that Jade was in the car behind and could only
watch horrified as the poor mutt was dragged 3 metres
along the tarmac. At first we thought Cody must be dead,
he looked such a mess lying there.

I leaned over him and pressed my fingers against
his throat. "He's still breathing!" I cried and, after scraping

him off the road, we rushed him to the nearest vets. Six months and 10,000 dollars later, he was starting to walk – and I mean literally, what with all his pins and rods and medical miracles. It was great to see him hobbling around again and worth every last penny, which is, unfortunately, exactly what the treatment cost us.

This financial blow was all the more bitter as we'd fallen in love with the house we were renting and were saving up to buy it. We'd both invested a lot of time in the property too – building walls, a bar and a pergola, and planting vegetables in the garden along with graceful palm trees. This was to be our own special paradise, a paradise on Earth.

Then came the second storm.

Despite help from my physiotherapists, Leanne and Beni, I'm still viewed as vegetative, yet mentally sharper, more aware of my surroundings and the day to day routine which invariably starts each morning with the droning of a Hoover. Half an hour later, the night shift nurses leave and the person looking after me for the day comes in to introduce him/herself - nice touch that - then breakfast, medications and, of course, the highlight of the morning – toileting!

I'm what they call 'full-hoisted' – in other words, I have to be lifted out of bed and transferred onto a commode shower chair by a hoist and full sling, which is harnessed at every corner so I can't fall out. There's one guy called Geoff who I particularly look forward to seeing because he makes me laugh. At the same time, he makes sure my fingers are straight and that I'm comfortable, so I trust him completely. But all the nurses are great here. Golden, you could say.

Once on the commode chair, I'm wheeled into the shower, enjoying the sensation while I exercise my head – still the only thing I can move the most, apart from my twitching thumb and one toe! During this process, I imagine I'm a boxer in training, like Rocky Balboa in the movie - another psychological trick which helps me cope with difficult situations like this, turning them into something heroic – at least until it comes to my 'bits'. Much to my despair, the nurses don't do under my foreskin as I would normally do and I can't use the alphabet board in the shower because it's not waterproof. Note to self – tell Jade. I just don't feel properly clean otherwise.

Minutes later, I'm fresh, dried and dressed in whatever the nurses choose for me. They always ask if I'm happy with their choice, although to be honest, I couldn't care less. I'm more bothered by the way my mouth keeps dribbling, mostly on my physiotherapists who keep trying - not always successfully - to catch each glob before it lands on their sleeves. So embarrassing – but then, if nothing except my head obeys me, what else can I expect from my bodily fluids?

With vet's bills, saving up for the house and taxes to pay, I couldn't afford to take time off, so when Jason went off on holiday for two weeks, I found work with a family friend, laying pipes – storm water pipes, sewage pipes, that sort of thing. It was a job I enjoyed and one that finished early, giving me more time for Jade and to work on the house. So all in all, life was pretty good.

Then one day, I stopped on the way to work for my regular Mocha fix. After paying, the shopkeeper was handing me my change when, all of a sudden, my eyes went fuzzy with stars as though I'd been rubbing my eyes too hard, and I went blind for several seconds. It worried me, of course, especially as the previous day I'd been almost knocked unconscious by a heavy blow on the back of the head from a sharp piece of concrete. But, typical ex-squaddie, I just shrugged it off with an, "Oh well!" and continued to work.

Fed, medicated, toileted, showered and dried. All present and correct, ready for the real work to begin. Physiotherapy starts with Leanne and Beni using a varnished timber slide board to ease me from my chair onto a plinth. This is to see if I can hold my balance in the adopted sitting position, a simple yet impossible task, as there's no way I can do it. Frustrated, I try over and over again but my body just keeps flopping to one side. Every day I hope to achieve it, yet every day I fail.

Jade is always here, always by my side, urging me on, encouraging me along with Mum and my sister and sometimes her husband Brad, while Leanne and Beni keep moving my fingers and the rest of my joints to stop them seizing up. I feel really silly, but no one seems to mind.

Sometimes, I'm put into a walking harness attached to the ceiling, and I just dangle on it, like a puppet on strings. My feet get sore being dragged along the floor, and the physios move my legs for me until my toes are scuffed, but there's nothing else for it but to grit my teeth, so to speak, and keep on trying. Not that I'm ever short of encouragement, of course; listening to the cheers of Jade and the rest of the Coghlan fan club, anyone'd think I was Usain Bolt!

I've had a trachea tube inserted to open my airway while, once every hour, a nurse pushes what feels like a giant straw down through my neck, pushing it straight into my lungs to suck out all the sticky, white phlegm which accumulates due to infection. Personally, I blame the cigarettes. Had I only known how disturbing it is to be coughing up litres of this disgusting stuff and watch the girl of my dreams trying to clean it up, I'd never have lit that first fag.

Chapter 7

I still have trouble swallowing. Robyn keeps spooning jelly into me, trying to trigger my throat muscles into action to help me speak. Recently, I finally managed a hearty gulp, much to the delight of Mum and Jade who'd been watching me for days; watching my mouth opening like a starving baby bird as the jelly swooped into sight.

Being able to swallow is apparently the most significant part of my recovery - a skill I'll never again take for granted! Since that first satisfying achievement, I've gone from strength to strength and can now take small swabs of liquid by mouth, which taste wonderful and refreshing. Next to Mum and Jade, Robyn has become my favourite person, bringing me iced water every day with different flavours to enjoy. What a treat! More importantly, these fluids help strengthen my swallowing muscles enough to have puréed food.

But there are still shocks and setbacks. One morning, I wake up unable to hear anything. "No! Not my hearing as well!" I groan inwardly and ring the bell for Geoff. "I a-m d-e—a-f," I spell out. "P-l-e-a-s-e c-h-e-c-k m-y e-a-r-s."

"No wonder you can't hear!" says Geoff, cheerfully, as he examines the offending orifices. "There's enough wax in there to polish a bus! Don't worry, Mate, we'll soon have it sorted." Sure enough, he unblocks my ears and I'm able to hear again. Clear as a bell.

But this isn't the only worry of the day. My cuff – a heart monitor shaped like a blue ball which is fixed to my chest - has started to deflate, a common problem, I believe, but none the less life-threatening; in fact, there's less than an hour for a new cuff to be inserted before the old one packs in completely! So here I am outside the operating theatre, feeling fainter and weaker as Mum and my sister Vicky hold my lifeless hands. I'm so tired, yet too scared to go to sleep in case I don't wake up again. My heart's beating louder and louder, while my chest constricts and

I'm struggling desperately to breathe. "This is it," I say to myself, "I'm dying, I'm really dying!" and it strikes me with awful irony that this should be happening now, just when I've come to accept my illness, just when I'm starting to fight back.

Next thing I know, it's early evening and I'm alone, sitting up in my wheelchair in front of a telly watching a football match. Heavily sedated, I can't quite remember why I'm in hospital. Then slowly, paranoia takes hold, twisting my thoughts; I come to the conclusion that everyone thinks I'm dead. It's all a conspiracy, yes, that's it! Geoff, the PCA, and his wife want to keep me here forever; to use me as some kind of pet or for some other fiendish purposes known only to themselves!

These wild imaginings are interrupted by Cherry, one of the nurses, who comes in to wipe my face and give me medication and, suddenly, with her reassuring presence, everything seems normal again, everything's okay, and I'm so relieved to be alive that all dark thoughts are disappearing, banished back to the abyss where they belong.

But after Cherry leaves, I start dwelling on things, about the life I had before, about my family and, most of all, my love for Jade. Ignoring the TV and its tiny men in shorts chasing round the pitch, I feel another wave of panic sweeping through my guts, tortuous doubts that make me question everything and everyone. What a horrible, sickening plot, I think - and Geoff and his wife seemed SUCH a nice couple!

They wheel me back to my room where, after being showered and dressed, I'm left in front of the TV again, watching re-runs of the Brady Bunch and trying to make sense of it all. Then Jade arrives and my heart springs back to life! Jade's here, Jade still loves me and all my negative thoughts and fears and panicky feelings just evaporate as I realise they were bollocks after all. I cry uncontrollably, but this time with relief.

Over the past few weeks, I've been suffering from a chesty cough which, thankfully, has all but disappeared. The doctors have been talking about removing my trachea tube – an awesome development. It was really weird having that tube inserted; coughing through my throat instead of my mouth made me feel like the Bionic Man – not a nice experience for visitors! Then one day, Jeremy, my male nurse, pulled it out – just pulled it out in front of loads of trainees! Ten of them there were, all standing around to watch how the procedure was done, and me lying lifeless, a human guinea pig. Amazing, though, how simple it was. They took out the tube, sealed the hole with a special plaster and left it.

Because the tube wasn't in that long, it only took about 14 days for my throat to heal up and it's hardly noticeable now, thanks to the expert medical crew along with lashings of Aloe Vera. I've been using this natural gel for 12 years - ever since my lymph node was removed during cancer treatment - and I'm certain it helps. You can hardly see the scar.

So here I am, less than three months after my brain stem stroke - less than three months after doctors at Sir Charles Gairdner's Intensive Care Unit told my family and my lovely Jade that I might never move again. I've no trachea tube anymore, my intravenous PICC line has been taken out and I no longer need a bag for my urine. All that remains, trailing tastefully from my nostril, is a feeding tube as I still can't eat food safely or swallow on command. This swallowing business is a major problem for me. I hate the way saliva dribbles constantly from my mouth – litres and litres of the stuff! But I keep practicing, trying to stimulate my throat muscles with Gollum-like gulps.

Then I concentrate on my vision - every night before sleep, retraining my eyes by looking around the ceiling as far as they move, following the ceiling contours slowly and deliberately. Unfortunately, this feat is almost impossible with a cocktail of drugs, which really gets me down at times. Okay, so my focus has improved and there's a little more movement in my neck. Every day, when Jade is by my side, I cry with frustration, horrified by the whole drama and generally feeling sorry for myself. But Jade stays strong. She never cries, does Jade. She never loses patience, and she never, ever lets me give up, encouraging me with even more experiences of people who've recovered from Locked-In Syndrome. That girl must spend hours on the internet tracking down every morsel of information she can. "This man drives a racing car now," she'll say. "You can do it, Pete! Be positive!" I want to be. I want my case to be like all these super humans Jade keeps on about, yet sometimes I just can't believe it will happen for me. It doesn't seem possible. I miss my life with Jade and hate this coffin of a body which keeps me from her.

Even so, I doubt I'll never get as low as I did in the early days at Sir Charles Gairdner, which must have been really hard for Jade, Mum and Vicky. At least they had an ally. Cora, a warm-hearted nurse from Germany, was absolutely ace, brilliant at dealing with miseries like me. She also knew how to use my alphabet board. One night, when I was feeling particularly low, I rang the head buzzer for her to come.

"I w-a-n-t t-o d-i-e." I spelled and fixed my eyes on her. For her part, Cora didn't make an issue of it, just smiled reassuringly.

"But you're doing so well, Peter. The doctors are really happy with you."

I sighed. Well, bully for them, I thought. I'M not happy! Besides, how could the doctors be happy when I couldn't even MOVE?

But then, after a mental audit, I realised that I HAD made progress, small though it was. And, of course, I had Jade. Jade was waiting for me and I had to get back to her. So I put the dark thoughts back in their box and, for the most part, they've stayed there. Thank God. And now I'm going to Shenton Park!

Strangely, despite being desperate to get there and convinced I'd make more headway with the physio

*department, when the time comes, I actually feel rather sad
to leave Charles Gairdner ward G51. Mum has brought in a
chocolate tree as a thank you, for Cora and the rest of the
staff, who've all lined up to see me off as I'm wheeled into a
waiting ambulance.*

*"Bye, Pete!" "Come back and see us!" Touched by their
warm sentiments, I remember how much they've all done
for me, from wiping my bum to showering, dressing and
feeding me. I was going to miss them, all of them. Wish I
could wave!*

*Five minutes in the ambulance and I'm about to
reach the next level in my fight against this nightmare. I
look out of the window as we speed past trees, wondering
what the nurses will be like, will they be as nice as Cora?
What sort of bed will I have? Will I make friends? And will
there be anyone there like me? This seems unlikely as, on
average, Shenton Park only has one LIS patient each year.*

*Not much longer to find out. The ambulance bucks
slightly over speed bumps as it approaches the
rehabilitation unit and slows to a halt. Then the back doors
swing open. I've arrived.*

Chapter 8

Shenton Park Rehabilitation Centre

To be honest, at first glance, Shenton Park is a bit of a let down. As I'm wheeled into my new ward, I'm reminded of the barracks from my army days - everything tired, faded and gloomy. I've been put into a single room where snot-green walls are chipped with nothing to brighten them except a picture of a surfboard on a beach. And the bed is hard, unlike the one at Charley's which had an air mattress.

The porter must have sensed my disappointment. "Temporary room, this," he says. "The main ward's being refurbished and won't be ready for another 6 months." When he leaves, my eyes are stinging with despair.

"Hi, my name's Steve. Welcome to Chateau Shents!" The young male nurse is friendly and has a strong Liverpool accent, again making me feel I'm back in the army. The last time I'd heard an accent like Steve's was in my regiment - the Cheshire Regiment; it was founded in Liverpool's Wirral peninsula and subsequently manned by Scousers and Mancs (Mancunians) like me.

"You okay mate?" he asks. Thank goodness for Jade. "The bed's too hard," she says. "Could we have an airbed, please?"

I feel pathetically dependent on Jade, like a small boy on his first day at school. All I want to do is stand up, to get on to my own two legs and walk out of here with my young lady. If only I could, I'd be running!

This place is a joke! I can't believe it's all happening –not again, not after everything. Not after my army ordeal and my fight with cancer. I'd come to Australia to start a new life, not to this... It seems hell will be my home for ever more!

By dinner time, Mum's here and she and Jade start feeding me with a spoon. At least one aspect of my life's improving. Now I can swallow more easily. I'm getting more used to puréed food, although a nurse has to supervise in case I choke on it. I hated that at first - made me feel like a baby and, even though I'm grateful, purée sucks!

Steve now takes me on a whistle-stop tour of the ward and adjoining corridor.

"This is the doctor's office. Here's the bathroom..." and so on. To hear him speak, you'd think it was Buckingham Palace instead of an old, decaying building with bile-coloured paintwork.

Once back in my room, Steve puts me to bed, turns on the TV and leaves me to it. I'm not interested in television. I'd rather be sitting at my bar drinking Scotch and coke with Jade, as I would normally do. And, to my surprise, I'm actually missing Charley's - my old room there, the staff, everything. So from trying to imagine what my first day will be like at Shenton Park, I'm now in the reality and I hate it. Professor Blacker was right, I DO need anti-depressants! I drift into my musings, praying for my life to change – and, most of all, for Jade to go on loving me.

"Don't dwell on things too much" Jade says, as she and Mum prepare to leave. Don't dwell on things? What else is there to do? She looks at my sullen expression and bends to kiss me goodbye. "It'll be alright, I promise!"

"Meds time!" Through the door of my new, old, miserable room comes a shaft of light in the form of Sam, a young New Zealander with a megawatt smile. "My name's Sam and I'll be giving you your medication," she says and immediately picks up the alphabet board. "Anything you want?" Sam is skilled at using the board and very patient with me as I blink out my concerns. I can't remember what I want to say, though, because we end up laughing so much. Sam makes me feel welcome and a little less scared. By the time my 'sleeper' starts to kick in, Shenton Park is definitely growing on me.

I wake up early, as usual, and span the ceiling to exercise my eyes. Then I focus on my hands, trying to improve the muscles in them, a process that takes me an hour or so. Considering I can hardly move, it's amazing how busy I am! And after ANY night's sleep I'm ready for anything. Just as well – every waking moment will be used to try and make some progress, try to get my body working, starting with my fingers.

Judy appears, a dainty girl with attractive Oriental looks who's also nifty with the alphabet board. As soon as she picks it up, I know I'm in good hands. Encouraged by her positive attitude, I pose the question which nobody to date has ever really answered.

"W-i-l-l I g-e-t b-e-t-t-e-r?" I blink. Judy pauses for a moment, considering me with gentle, almond eyes.

"Well why else would you be here?" she replies. "Tell you what we're going to do - first of all, we'll get you into your chair more often, that helps your core muscles."

"A-r-e y-o-u C-h-i-n-e-s-e?" I ask. Judy rewards me with a smile.

"Yes, I came to Australia with my folks when I was a baby - good guess. Most people think I'm Japanese!"

I click with Judy straight away. It's nice to be chummy with the person who gives me my shower! Judy and another nurse transfer me to a shower commode and wheel me to the bathroom – predictably old and dreary like the rest of the place. Once clean and dry, I'm hoisted back onto the bed to be dressed by two nurses who work in pairs so as not to hurt me or damage their backs in the process. They promise I'll get a timetable tomorrow once they've done a few checks.

"Hi!" I turn to see a slim, young woman entering the room. "I'm your Physiotherapist and I intend to keep you very busy while you're here with us."

"Better believe it, Matey!" says Judy, "She may look dainty but Alisha is a regular Sergeant Major in the gym!"

I gaze at this pretty, fair-haired, lady as she examines my legs, searching for any sign, any ray of hope, any glimmer of reaction in her steady light eyes. Could she get me moving again? Eager though I am to get cracking, I can't think what can possibly be done with my lifeless, useless body; there's nothing to work on but twitchy knees, a thumb that only budges 5 millimetres and a couple of toes that move even less!

But whether she feels I'm a lost cause or not, Alisha's far too professional to give anything away. Her attitude is positive and her smile reassuring.

"Right!" she exclaims decisively. "I'll see you in the gym, then."

Next to introduce herself is Joslyn, a dark-haired, green-eyed lady who tells me she's my Occupational Therapist, here to measure me up for a new chair. It's going to be made by Rehab Engineering so I'm expecting something supersonic! After Joslyn, a nurse comes in wanting to swab my ass for any infections I might have picked up from Charley's. Apparently, there was an outbreak of something earlier in the month, so this embarrassing process will need to be repeated for the next three days at least!

Now doctors join the queue, testing my knee and elbow reflexes and prodding parts of my body with bits of plastic, sharp and blunt in turn, to see if I can feel the difference. One doctor examines my eyes, asking me to follow her finger; up, down, right to left until I'm going cross-eyed. All this attention makes me feel like a guinea pig, but hey! They're just doing their job.

When Jade, Mum and Vicky turn up, they're surprised by all the activity, seeing as they were told I wouldn't have any therapy today. They're also dismayed at my determined glumness, having hoped the change to a new environment would buck me up a bit. The letters I spell out put paid to that.

"W-h-e-n w-i-l-l t-h-i-s b-e o-v-e-r?" I blink, "I w-a-n-t m-y o-l-d l-i-f-e b-a-c-k! I h-a-t-e t-h-i-s s-h-i-t!" Then I get all maudlin. "I l-o-v-e y-o-u" "I m-i-s-s y-o-u" etcetera, etcetera, while the tears start streaming. All I want is to move on and, until I do, I'm unable to think of anything – or anyone – else.

Suddenly, a man appears at the door, a well-built man, in his fifties I'd guess, with spectacles. Oh, and an electric chair which he powers towards me. "Don't cry, mate!" he urges. There's kindness in his voice, despite his blokey manner.

"Name's John," he continues. "Not too long ago I was just like you, lozzing around feeling sorry for myself. And now look! I'm sitting up, getting about and STILL feeling sorry for myself!" he laughs, "but not as much! It teaches you something when you're in this state, something really unique."

Turns out he lives just around the corner from mine and Jade's house and ended up here after a stroke. He then went on to tell us how it happened, when and why, and about all the improvements he's made, and I'm listening intently, trying to catch a little of his optimism.

Another thing we have in common – he used to be in the army and is no stranger to combat, having endured two tours of Vietnam.

"Survive two of those, you'll survive anything!" he says. "And you didn't do so badly either – living in Northern Ireland." He leans towards me and lowers his voice.

"It takes guts to be a soldier, doesn't it?" I blink in agreement. "Tell you what, though, Pete. It takes even more guts to face what you're going through right now. But you'll do it, I can tell, because you're determined, I see it in your eyes. You're a fighter, like me. So keep going lad - be patient and things will change, I promise you."

These are words I desperately need to hear, words which miraculously turn off my tear ducts. I must confess, though, to a twinge of jealousy. John's stroke was one-sided, so he can still do all the things I want to do: eat, sleep, talk and wipe my own ass. Simple things we take for granted – until we can't do them anymore. Like now, for instance; before John wheels himself away, I want to ask if he'll pop by again but, as I blink towards the alphabet board, he pre-empts my request. Pausing at the door, he swivels his chair around to face me.

"Know what I reckon? I reckon you and me are a force to be reckoned with! Can't wait for you to move in!" Seeing my puzzled expression, John laughs. "Didn't they tell you? Apparently you'll be joining me in the barracks – well, me and two others - but I'll look after you. It'll be fun!"

"T-h-a-n-k-s." In reply, John smiles and then he disappears, his chair squeaking its way up the corridor.

A few hours later, a nurse called Ben is taking me to have a look-see at these 'barracks', a four-man room with a bed in each corner. I'm overwhelmed by it all and, despite John's rallying call, burst out crying. Ben holds the alphabet board for me: "I j-u-s-t w-a-n-t m-y a-r-m-s."

"Course you do," says Ben, with the same positive tone Judy used earlier, "that's why you're *here*." He gestures to one of the beds. "The last guy here couldn't use his arm, either. But know what? When he left the other day, he was waving to us all!" This gives me a bit of hope and I stop crying, leaving Ben to dry my eyes and wipe the snot away.

Chapter 9

Ben and I have become really good friends. He's quite a card, cracking jokes, making me laugh and sending texts for me to Jade – which I insist on checking just in case he gets cheeky! He also looks out for me when inexperienced agency nurses are trying to hoist me in and out of bed. Some of these nurses are very nice, of course, do their job well and all that - but I can only speak from a patient's point of view.

When you're locked-in, helpless and vulnerable, there's nothing more worrying and frustrating than an agency nurse who doesn't know you, who fails to take your condition into account. If the bed isn't exactly the way you want it, it causes all sort of misery. Someone able-bodied can at least change position if they need to; for patients who are totally paralysed like me, that isn't an option.

Little things take on huge proportions. One of my concerns is that there's always a pillow at the bottom of my bed to stop me getting drop-foot; I also need to have my hands on top of the covers, the way I like them. A *regular* nurse learns to read your expressions, to know without asking when you want to use the alphabet board or need an extra pillow. People who can't move or talk simply can't cope with spelling everything out to someone different every night.

For example, I woke up on one occasion desperate for the loo. Having called for the agency nurse on duty, I spelled out my need for a bedpan (like a potty, but to lie on), so off she went and came back with a big, round, green pan that was too hard for my bony butt. Regular nurses are aware that I always have the slipper pan, which is comfier and doesn't leave bruising.

But this is a detail the agency nurse couldn't possibly have been aware of. Or maybe she failed to read my care plan. By the time she realises her mistake, I'm

bursting, so much so that halfway through spelling out my problem, I can't hold it any longer and crap the bed, something I haven't done for weeks. Infuriated by this undeserved and unnecessary humiliation, I'm making an earnest request to health professionals:
PLEASE, *PLEASE* DON'T ASSIGN AGENCY NURSES TO LOCKED-IN PATIENTS UNLESS REGULAR!

On the plus side, I now have a staunch ally in Ben and Steve, who pop in when on duty, even if they're assigned to a different room. I was beginning to feel safe with my wards 'REGULAR' carers, who genuinely consider my needs. This makes a world of difference, as it would to any locked-in sufferer, providing peace of mind as well as a comfortable night's sleep. I'm also blessed in having my family around. They've typed out lists for the nurses detailing my likes and dislikes.

And now I have two new survivor allies: John and Craig.

Having moved into the barracks, I've found John, the Vietnam vet, as good as his word. He and his fellow inmate Craig looks out for me constantly, making sure the nurses keep me upright in my chair so I'm not lolling helplessly to one side.

Already, we've established a good routine. John has an early shower then helps to raise me up on my electric bed before grabbing his favourite beverage, Cappuccino - one for himself and one for Craig. Craig's a real coffee addict and a genuinely nice guy who gives me honey for my porridge every morning. Much as I'd love to, the morning coffee ritual is something I can't yet follow, being restricted to fluids of 400 level thickness for my safety. Coffee would only end up being aspirated down the wrong hole and causing an infection like pneumonia, something I can very well do without!

As it happened, I've been infected anyway – four times! – thanks to a temporary resident to our ward, a cheeky guy who arrived just after me. He swears. He swears a lot. He also has speech problems in that he talks gibberish most of the time, but thinks he's making sense as he fires questions at me in his own curious language, spoken with the gravity of a seasoned TV newscaster.

"Yaba daba doo?" he'll say, or something of the sort, and then he cocks his head to one side, waiting for an answer as if I know what the blazes he's talking about! I'm ashamed to admit it, given my own speech problems, but he makes me laugh. The incomprehensible meets the unutterable!

No doubt about it, Zoomer's certainly livened things up! I've nicknamed him Zoomer due to the speed he cranks up on his regular bids for freedom. Despite being told repeatedly to stay in our room, Zoomer tries to escape every chance he gets - at least three times every dinner break – frantically propelling his wheelchair backwards with his one good leg, determined to outpace the nurses in a desperate bid for a smoke. He never succeeds, though, thanks to beady-eyed nurses who lurk around every corner and usually catch him well before he reaches the exit. As they wheel him back to the ward for the umpteenth time that day with resigned expressions on their faces, Zoomer swears at them in frustration, but always with an engaging grin that sets me off laughing all over again. So much so, it almost kills me!

Back from physio, I'm getting a pain in my right lower ribs but my first reaction is to brush it aside. "Probably indigestion," I think, having made a pig of myself at lunch – but then it's so good to be able to eat *anything* after weeks of pap, who can blame me?

Anyway, I spell it out to Jade after she's wheeled me back from physio and she mentions it to the nurse. No more ado, I'm heading for the X-ray department – on a bed, would you believe? – which hacks me off big time, as the dramatic way I've been spirited away gets everybody worrying about me. Besides, Jade only has an hour to spend with me and we were looking forward to watching 'Shameless' together on telly; coming from North West England, we love hearing the accents!

Anyway, Joe, the Spanish nurse, manages to cheer me up, as he always does and gets me into the X-ray department, next in the queue. The Radiographer there looks at me blankly. "What are you here for?" she asks, so I just stare back at her until she realises her mistake.

"Ooops!" she said, as she finally cottons on. "Sorry, you can't talk, can you?" A young girl comes round the corner and calls my name. Instinctively, I try to answer, "Here!", but of course nothing comes out. All I can do is nod and form the word with my mouth. "One day!" I think.

So now they sit me up and place this dark foam triangle behind me, take all their X-rays and lie me down again ready for Joe to collect me and return me to the ward. "Load of fuss about nothing," I'm thinking, and then, blow me, back come the results and I've got pneumonia! I must have inhaled food or fluid, probably due to laughing so much at Zoomer and his antics!

Back on a drip again, this time for antibiotics which means having a cannula inserted. Now, after all my cancer treatment I should be used to needles – by the time I'd finished chemo, I had more holes than a crop sprinkler! Unfortunately, the chemotherapy has caused my veins to thin, so the nurses have problems getting into the vein, causing heavy bleeding or, at the very least, a lot of discomfort.

Worse than that, when it finally gets flowing, the machine beeps annoyingly for 30 minutes, which, seeing as I have to be infused 3 times a day, irritates me and my room mates no end! The first dose is administered really early in the morning, the second at lunchtime and the third after dinner when we want to watch telly. But, mustn't grumble – the antibiotics are doing the trick. In fact, the staff's rapid response to my 'stitch' has undoubtedly saved my life!

For the sake of any LIS sufferers who are reading this, I cannot express just how dangerous it is when food or drink goes down the 'wrong way'. This often happens as the result of uncontrollable laughter - a common side-effect of a stroke, which is why my eating has to be carefully monitored. In fact, I have to eat in the TV room away from my room mates or anyone else who can make me laugh. One look at Zoomer, for instance, with his self-propelling leg, and my hysteria sets in, causing me to choke or aspirate on the soggy mince I usually get for tea.

As far as staff are concerned, there's only one solution – for me to be supervised at all times. A member of staff watches from the doorway as Jade or one of my family feeds me, and woe betide me if I attempt to laugh. Even a smile earns me a look of stern disapproval. For a 32-year old man who has been round the world, served in the army and done more in a short life than most, it's a humiliating experience which fills me with rage. I just want to jump out of my wheelchair and scream the place down.

Seriously, I've had enough. Every night I wear myself out trying to strengthen whatever will wiggle or flex, trying to make my weakened, ravaged body MOVE! I'm mad and I'm NOT going to stay like this!

In physio or when alone in the garden, I'm constantly moving my arm forward and backwards on my lap tray, albeit an inch on a slide sheet, angrily determined to get my arm strong again. Strange that I'm usually the only one doing this, for most patients, physio is enough. Not for me though, I need more than 2-3 gym sessions. I want to be exercising every chance I get. Me? I'm checking out of Chateau Shents A.S.A.P!

When it comes to speech, of course, I'm doing my best to make improvements. Just as well I've a really good Speech Therapist in David, a handy-looking guy in his 40s with eyes that make me chuckle when he smiles trying his best to be professional. At my first assessment, he asked me to say "Aaaaaaaaa" and "Mooooooo" a few times, which I just about managed but with very little sound. He didn't say much, just left me with some exercises to do.

Then there's Wayne, my dietician who, after introducing himself, told me there'd be no choosing my own food, as I was on a moist, minced diet, but that he'd try to help vary it for me if he could. He seems pretty cool although I haven't seen much of him since.

And then there is my new physiotherapist, Alisha who is waiting to conduct my first session at the gym. As I arrive in my wheelchair pushed by an orderly, Alisha greets me with a friendly grin and lets me watch for a while as other patients are put through their paces, doing loads of different exercises; moving plastic cones, reaching for balloons, sitting, standing – all moving to some degree in order to recover their strength and mobility.

Seeing how focused they are, I'm struck with a painful reality. None of them are nearly as helpless as me. I'm the most disabled patient here by far – the only one with an alphabet board. My heart sinks as my eyes search around the room, desperate to spot someone else with a board like mine but, no, I'm the only one.

Alisha manoeuvres me onto a plinth, just as Leanne and Benny have done so many times at Charley's. She wants to see if can sit up unaided, which I manage for a second or two before keeling over like a skittle. Next, she turns her attention to my hands and feet, extending them to their full limit to stop them seizing up. She chats to me all the time to let me know what she's doing and why.

I'm now put in a sitting position again while Alisha works on my back, lifting it from its now permanent slouch so I'm raised up as though about to eat a meal. This, she explains, will not only work my back muscles but get my brain used to the movement again. As she continues with the exercise, I spot a small red gnome wearing sunglasses grinning at me from a shelf nearby. Its jolly appearance seems totally out of place here – it must have been a gift. My eyes then drift to strategically placed posters; one says, "The Department of Silly Walks" and another urges us to "Never Give Up."

Having finished stretching my extremities, Alisha has me hoisted onto the tilt table which is angled until I'm in a standing position strapped in tightly. It feels good to be upright again after so many months - this table is definitely my favourite bit of kit! Being upright means Alisha can work on me while my body weight forces my ankles to sit in a normal position, stretching my ham strings and also helping me eventually support my weight.

Finally, air splints are applied to try and straighten my arms which are currently bent into and across my chest. These long splints are put on my arms and then inflated so they'll keep my arms straight, a bit like armbands!

Session over and the rest of the day passes as all the rest do with toileting, feeding, meds, sleeping. Whether it's all the exercise I've had, I don't know, but I'm sleeping better now, except for the way my hands keep rising to my throat, like I'm in some kind of horror movie. And I can't push them away.

Fortunately, Alisha listened patiently as I blinked out my request I came up with an idea! "I want sandbags on my wrists at night, Alisha. They'll keep my arms by my sides."

The sandbags work fine, but it's hell at first, making me feel like Hannibal Lecter. Awful, but I'm put at ease knowing my hands aren't going throttle me. A great win! Alisha was sent to me for sure.

Chapter 10

Horrible night; I can't sleep because of the storm, and these sandbags on my wrists are heavy! If I could toss and turn I would, but all I can do is lie here, listening as the rain lashes against the windows, washing in all kinds of uninvited guests.....

One of which is crawling up my arm!

Swivelling my eyes, I expect to see a spider, which would be bad enough. But this is worse! A red millipede, an absolute monster, two inches long at least, and it's heading for my face! Frantically, I ring the buzzer with my head - three times for Emergency!

The nurse comes running and picks up my alphabet board. All I really want to do is scream, but instead, I have to keep one eye on the monster while trying to spell "m-i-l-l-i-p-e-d-e". I give up and just blink the word "s-p-i-d-e-r" instead and the nurse's face turns whiter than chalk! "S-p-i-d-e-r a-r-m l-o-o-k," I spell, but by now it's gone round the back of my neck so the nurse can't see it at first. Gingerly, she pulls down the sheets, one at a time, no doubt hoping it's all in my imagination. But no! Now she sees it crawling on my chest and screams at the top of her voice, loudly enough for the both of us. "Oh God!"

Brave woman! Face contorted with disgust and fear, she manages to snatch it up and throw it into the waste bin, quickly covering it over with a board to stop the monster escaping. Catastrophe averted!

After last night's thrilling activities, I'm totally useless in the gym. I so want to work hard, but my treacherous body just won't let me!

On the plus side, my Dad's arrived from Thailand with his lovely wife, Noi. They first came to see me during the early stages of my illness, which I barely remember. I've just three vague recollections of their visit; Noi holding my shoulder when I couldn't see anything, and Dad's immortal words as he watched me being wheeled into my first room at Charley's. "Good fans, them." Then someone turned on the TV and asked what channel I wanted and Dad said, "The news - he likes the news." Typical of my Dad. Faced with the gut-churning sight of his only son, twisting violently in spasms; unable to help, powerless to stop me rapidly diminishing before his very eyes, he managed to keep a lid on things. He talked about electric fans ... and news bulletins.

But today, things are different. Today, he and Noi come to watch me in physio; me standing upright on the tilt table, Dad standing proud, nodding encouragingly yet looking on with the same concerned expression he had after taking the stabilisers off my bike. It was a caring Dad who'd watched me peddle away those twenty-odd years ago, my five-year old legs pumping nineteen to the dozen. It's a caring Dad who's looking out for me now.

The bad news is he and Noi are only here for a week. Dad's a busy man these days, having built up a construction business, providing luxury homes for expats to the rural farmlands of Chomburi, Thailand - an absolute paradise and somewhere I'd like to live too. But while they're here, they intend to spend as much time with me as possible.

Noi turns out to be a real help. After my therapies for the day, she massages my arms and legs, then starts cleaning and filing my nails, a meticulous process which Thai people believe helps the nerves re-connect after strokes. Naturally, I'm all for it, desperate for any shred of hope, although I do feel a bit of a girl with all this pampering! Dad sits and watches like a hawk, literally *willing* me well again!

"It's only a matter of time, Son," he insists. "The brain has to re-wire itself." I hope he's right.

Actually, pathetically weak though it is, my arm does seem to have slightly more movement, but whether this is due to physio, Noi's expert manicure, or my wishful thinking, I'll never know. While Dad's here, I ask the nurse to pass me my lap-tray so I can practice pushing my arms around on it. Incidentally, when doing this exercise, I need to have a slide sheet which moves me up the bed, making it far easier to move my arms which would otherwise be far too heavy and stick to the tray. A slide sheet also stimulates movement should there be any sign of it.

I can move my arms forward a bit, but not outwards, which really worries me. If I can only move my arms in all directions – just a fraction – then I could build on that.

For now, I have to put my faith in all the other treatments on Shenton's programme. Every day, I have speech therapy, occupational therapy and physio and I'm also about to go into the hydrotherapy pool for exercises. Sounds really hopeful.

Alisha is already waiting for me as I'm wheeled into the pool area. By means of a slide board, two of the staff attach a safety float to my neck, position me onto a transport bed and lower me into the water.

"Relax, Pete", says Alisha. "You're quite safe. I'm going to take you sea-weeding." Sea-weeding involves floating me up and down the pool with a snake-like, sweeping, side-to-side motion.

"This will help loosen your spine," Alisha explains. "Water removes weight and gravity, so it makes it easier for your body to start moving again." The swishing of the water beneath me certainly feels good, and my spine seems to yield slightly along with the rest of my body.

Jade, of course, has a poolside seat and I wonder what she must be thinking as she observes her fiancé floating back and to in front of her, aware that her dreams, like mine, have been cruelly flushed away. Distressed by these thoughts, I stare upwards at the tounge and groove timber ceiling - hopeless, helpless and extremely vulnerable.

For a few seconds, I imagine I'm swimming in Dad and Noi's pool in Thailand, feeling the hot sun caressing my skin. I imagine thrusting through the water and try to move my arms from my chest. But they're no match for the gentle current. Alisha holds my arms. "Try to bend your wrists, Pete."

I can't.

I had such high hopes of electric stimulation and this magic hydrotherapy pool, expecting to see instant results. In actuality, during my first weeks it seems I'll just be floating about. What can I do? Just how can I get my body working again?!

And now, the session is over. I'm hauled out of the water, settled into my chair and swaddled in towels to prevent me getting pneumonia while Jade pushes me back to my room for a shower. This irritates me, as it cuts into my time with Jade who, after finishing work, has to watch me floating for an hour and then wait around until I've been showered. The short time we have left together is spent over dinner, with Jade spoon-feeding me before leaving to see to our dog, Cody. All I want is to be with her; to have quality time with the girl I love instead of being dragged around from pillar to post.

Fortunately, I've found a sympathetic ear. From now on, my shower time will be changed and on pool days I won't have one at all. All I want is some quality time with Jade.

After all, no one could call me a shirker. Day after day, week after week, I've been 100% committed to my therapies – continuing them on my own for hours after the sessions. Even at night I'm at work, trying to improve my speech by sticking out my tongue and stretching it as far as it will go. I've also been told that smiling and frowning will strengthen my face muscles, so this is what I do as I lie in bed, the old visage grimacing and gurning for all it's worth – like an All Black player doing the Maori Haka!

When I had a room of my own, I'd try to form the words, "How are you?" "Hello," "Goodbye" and "I love you," thinking if I practiced for long enough I could make myself understood. Since then, I've learned that the soft pallet at the roof of my mouth isn't working properly; air is expelled from my nose instead of my mouth, making it virtually impossible to pronounce the letters "b", "p", "s" or "t". Come to that, I can't pronounce anything else much either because, during my spell on life support in ICU, my lungs got used to minimal breathing, leaving my chest muscles too weak to push any air through my voice box. So, no matter how much effort I put in, I never get anything out it seems!

But there's one goal I've achieved quite easily. Too easily! I've been eating as much as I can to regain some of my weight, increasing from a skinny 63 kilos to 80 kilos. No doubt, I'd have gone on to break the record (as well as my wheelchair!) had one of the nurses not warned me about a man who got so fat it affected his ability to walk. That's enough for me. From now on, I'm only going to eat healthy stuff and give my puddings away!

I'm trying to explain to Mum and Jade why I can't indulge in that delicious chocolate mousse on my tray, when we hear singing from the corridor. It's a group from a local church giving their vocal chords an airing for the benefit of the patients. Normally, I hate churchy songs but, desperate for any kind of hope, I ask to be wheeled out to listen. Moved by the music, I feel the all too familiar tears welling in my eyes and start to blink. "I j-u-s-t w-a-n-t m-y h-a-n-d-s t-o w-o-r-k." The singing lasts for another fifteen minutes or more and I continue to listen, the tears now running freely, scalding down my cheeks.

I've never believed in God. But right now it'd be good to know there's somebody up there. Somebody looking out for me. Someone who cares.

So, I decide: "If you *do* exist, God, you and me are going to have a chat." So here goes! Once settled for the night, lying in the darkness with not a sound to be heard other than John and Craig snoring, I quietly introduce myself to the Almighty. And then, for the first time in my life, I start to pray.

"Please God, please listen to me. I know I'm not the best person in the world, I mean, I've never been one for church, and I'm certainly no choir boy, but maybe you'll overlook that for now, just for now. You see, there's nobody else I can turn to now and I'm running out of hope. All I want is to move again, to be like I was, with Jade. That's all I want. So please, please God, if you're there, help me start moving; help me make some progress. Please! And if you do, and if I can just move my hand, just a bit, I'll know you've heard me.

'Tell you what, I'll do a deal with you. If I can get better..., I mean if you *help* me get better..., I promise I'll help others for the rest of my life, especially others like me; because you know what God, being like this has made me see there's too much pain in the world. And if it hurts *me* to see it, a godless, booze-swilling, fag-smoking, ex-squaddie, then it's *got* to hurt You! So please, please God, if you exist, if you can hear me then help me, please! Please, please help me!"

Whether God has listened to me or not, I made a deal that day!

Chapter 11

Believe it or not, two weeks after my initial heart to heart with the Almighty, one of my arms has started working! There it was at the side of my lap-tray, my hand dangling from the end of it, as I try for the umpteenth time to wiggle my fingers in a Mexican wave and, suddenly, it's like being plugged into an electric socket, with a familiar surge of energy pumping life into me. My hand is actually moving! The fingers are wiggling! Still weak, still imperfect, but fully opened like never before, until I can even use a laptop. Moving the cursor is difficult, and I do find it hard to push down the keys, but wow!

A world of activity is now within my grasp. Slowly over weeks I learn to brush my own teeth, blow my own nose and just about wash my own hair! Never again will I say there is no God! Truth be told, I *had* hoped for a miracle, to be catapulted out of my wheelchair straight away! The reality was I'd been handed dignity back; the gift of touch!

I work on my arm every night after therapy, tensing whatever muscle I can, maximising any flicker my biceps and triceps can muster. My next Herculean task... grabbing hold of the covers, lifting them off me and putting them back! A light exercise for some, yet to me, the light cotton sheets might just as well be reinforced concrete.

Bench pressing my sheets - just ridiculous!

Another part of my bedtime routine is to stretch an elastic physio band which is tied to the safety rail of my bed. Ten minutes every night before sleep or while waiting for the nurses morning hand-over have done wonders for my left arm. It feels so much stronger now.

In fact, I'm a real glutton for exercise these days. Come evening, I'm lying starkers on the bed, no covers, iPod in full-blast as I tense my legs and arms, anything to get those neural pathways firing! (Opening my curtains round my bed could be quite traumatising for unsuspecting visitors!)

When Jade's here, she puts a pillow at the bottom of my bed which I try to push downwards with my feet and Mum's brought me a Grip Master – a device that I squeeze to strengthen my grip – along with some 1k weights to build up my biceps. Holding the weights, I try twisting my wrists in a circular motion, then up and down over my lap-tray. I've noticed these movements are easier when my hands are tensed up, so I use a sweat band to hold them in a tight fist, preventing my fingers from opening to keep hold of the weight.

I can also lift my legs, an inch from the bed, and this is something I do as many times as I can before going to sleep, lifting them over and over again until they hurt. For added motivation, I work to the rhythm of the iPod which Jade bought for me. Any music with a beat – euphoric trance, rock, hip hop, metal – helps get me through the pain barrier and keeps me focused. Through constant exercising and sheer determination, I'm progressing, getting a little more supple, a little more mobile, a lot more hopeful day by day!

My advancement hasn't gone unnoticed by the medical profession either. Recently, I was invited to attend a meeting for neurologists in Perth, none of whom have ever known a locked-in patient to recover this quickly. My own specialist, Professor Blacker, took me into the lecture hall and introduced me. Overwhelmed, I looked up to see over 50 doctors in attendance, all staring with awed expectation as I lifted my good arm.

"Could you raise your left leg for us, Peter?" Professor Blacker asked. Obligingly, I managed a kick that David Beckham would envy to be rewarded by a nod of satisfaction from Professor Blacker. He paused for maximum effect.

"Peter..." he announced, "...is also regaining his speech." Again, everyone looked at me, waiting for the miracle, so I wished them all, "Good morning," in my soft nasal voice. I'd been practicing.

Stunned silence! Unnerved, I glanced down to make sure my flies weren't undone but I needn't have worried. Within seconds, the lecture hall erupted in ecstatic applause; so much so, I looked around expecting to see the Queen arriving. But no, it was all for me! I backed away in my wheelchair, shy of the attention, and headed for the nearest corner where I hoped to sit out the rest of the session without any further embarrassment. Professor Blacker smiled at me encouragingly; then, to my great relief, switched to a lengthy slide show presentation on the inner workings of my brain. Talk about exposure!

Of course, I didn't have a clue what he was on about. The Professor's voice faded into the background as I gazed longingly out of the window and beyond the fields to distant traffic.

"Will I ever get out there again?" I wondered. I also wondered why the doctors were making such a fuss of me. Okay, maybe it isn't normal for people to recover quite so quickly, but it still seems ruddy slow to me, especially as I'm literally working every second of the day. No one could be more focused, or more determined, or spend more time trying to get well.

All I want now is to get back to physio where I can push myself further. I'm there as often as I can be, even when it's not on my timetable – which is three hours in the morning and two hours in the afternoon after speech or occupation therapy. I also do another three hours at night and a couple more hours before hand-over in the morning, naked. Poor nurses! They work pretty well around the clock. Thank goodness for Alisha – I'm sure she works overtime with me, yet she never complains.

Wish I was as keen on occupation therapy but it's very frustrating. I fail at virtually everything the therapist asks me to do, simply because my fingers aren't so clever. One exercise is to hold a prickly ball under each hand and see if I can keep them from rolling off. I manage for roughly a minute before my hands flop off.

Perhaps it's psychological. At my first session, one of the OT staff told me I'd never get the use of my arms back 100%, which devastated me and set me off crying for hours.

Eventually, my tears turned to anger and I grew more determined than ever to get myself back on form. "Come on, Cogs!" I said to myself, "Since when did you ever give in?" From then on, I started concentrating all the more on forcing my arms to function.

I now have one arm moving 100% and the other 50%, and I'll have them both up to scratch one day – just watch me! I believe that believing is achieving and that if you try your hardest, you can do anything. Once the nerves are reconnected, then it's all down to you.

Already, the OT people are amazed at how well I've advanced, saying they've never seen an arm come back so quickly, which just goes to show, they can't always predict results. They certainly underestimated *me*! And what many people have failed to realise is the amount of effort I've put in – almost every second of every day is devoted to getting well again, to getting back to ME!

Maybe their initial prognosis has helped fire me up, so has proved a good thing in a way. All the same, I wish they'd spared me their initial crippling opinions, and said something noncommittal like, "Well that's why you're here!" or, "I think if we work really hard together, anything is possible!" instead of the dreadful pronouncement: "I've seen your type of case before," and passing me a tissue, a memory that vexes me even now. From that point on I've never really put faith in them. In fact, I've begun to hate occupational therapy because it depresses me so much. Can't people understand? All I want is to be normal!

And now, my stomach muscles have started to kick in! I'm lying on the tilt table during physio, when a university student called Tim lowers the table back by about 10 degrees. "Can you move forward a bit?" he asks. I doubt it, but am prepared to try and, because I'm nearly upright anyway, manage to move about 3 inches! I laugh with jubilation. So these muscles *can* work – all they need now is building up from scratch!

Now I know what can be achieved, there's no stopping me. Three inches become five inches, and five inches become ten until, three months later – three months of agonisingly hard work, exercising my stomach for half an hour a day - I can sit up 50% from the tilt table. That's equivalent to a half sit-up! Alisha is delighted, yet doesn't let me rest on my laurels. "There's more to getting better than just using your stomach." She says, and gets me on the bike.

At first, it's hard to peddle as every time I get it going, resistance kicks in. One of the physios called Pete comes up with a brainwave. "How's about setting the distance monitor? That way you can keep up a nice, flat, steady pace so you can keep going longer."

Much better! Once I get used to it I'm able to peddle for about half an hour, although it takes several weeks just to reach one measly kilometre! But I keep pushing myself until I can do three kilometres, then ten, then twenty – so Alisha puts up a record sheet for me! "Where's my gold star?" I demand, and she just smiles.

Alisha tickles me. Literally! She's spending a lot of time this session on my bad arm which otherwise gets quite stiff, stretching it and massaging my tendon around my armpit. Unfortunately, I'm extremely ticklish there and I laugh hysterically. The whole gym is watching me, wondering what a strokie like me could possibly find so funny – but, as everyone knows in Chateau Shenton, laughter is my best medicine. In fact, I'm notorious for it, having been thrown off the ward numerous times for laughing.

Like the time I was in a toilet cubicle and I heard a man saying: "Quick! I'm going to s*** myself!" then seconds later: "It's coming, it's coming!" and then: "Oh shit!" I shouldn't have laughed, I know, but after being in the same predicament myself more times than I care to remember on transfer, I'd come to see the funny side of it. Problem was, what started out as a sympathetic chuckle got louder and louder until I was a shrieking donkey. Apparently, hysterical laughter is common in recovering strokies.

On my wall is a picture of my beloved Nanna waving at me, who's no longer around. Even so, I talk to her sometimes, convinced, that if she's aware of anything at all, she'd be watching me, willing me on! She's with me, I just know it.

Chapter 12

"Life is like a box of chocolates; you never know what you're gonna get," said Forest Gump. Well, me, I got the f***ing lot, or so it seems. But I'll keep carrying on, keep on smiling. I've come this far and, God knows how much further I'll get, but one thing's for sure - I'm not giving up. Not yet. If there's one thing I've learned from this wretched business, it's to take no notice of worst case scenarios – the experts aren't always right!

In between therapy sessions and visits from Jade and the family, I've had plenty of time to mull things over. Have I been lucky or unlucky in life? I've certainly had plenty of shocks - you know, the type of "Whatever next?" events your average person rarely experiences. Maybe it's the emphasis on physical training here at Shenton. Maybe it's because certain incidences in my past run deeper than I've realised, particularly during my army days.

I vividly recall one particular marching season in Dunloy, Northern Ireland, a perilous time when Protestant Orangemen paraded through the streets in defiance of Catholic Republicans. Let's just say it was rare for such marches to end peacefully, which is why me and fellow soldiers were squashed in the back of an army vehicle, ready to assist the RUC officers on the frontline trying to quell the riots.

Being nowhere near the action, we weren't in any danger (so we thought) and were sitting pretty not far away and actually rather bored, what with all the waiting around. Eventually our commander came over to give us a briefing. He'd just opened the door to our vehicle when a petrol bomb came flying out of nowhere in his direction. Someone yelled and he immediately jumped out of the way before the glass exploded right by our vehicle with us still inside, so close we could smell burning from our hair and eyebrows! Later, we learned a couple of terrorists had sneaked round the back of the terraced houses nearby, cutting through the gunnels to reach their target.

Two years later, I was again in the firing line – with an even more determined enemy. It was my 21st birthday and I was diagnosed with Hodgkin's Lymphoma. At least it got me out of the army!

Yet for sheer unmitigated horror, nothing, nothing I've ever encountered compares with being locked-in! Nothing even comes close. Once again, I brace my mind ready to resume my journey.

Every day, I'm becoming more focused, more determined, with rarely a tear and scarcely a trace of self-pity. I'm more independent too and, though still in need of hoisting to the bed and the loo, can now drive myself to therapy in my electric chair. I can almost feed myself (though things tend to get a bit messy!), clean my teeth with an electric toothbrush and, best of all, text Jade to tell her how much I love her and miss her. Having regained the use of one arm has changed the whole ball game! Being transferred to Shenton has certainly benefitted me and, apparently, I'm Lucky, as not every patient gets the chance to come here? It's only through the recommendation of Professor Blacker that I'M here. So in answer to my previous question, I'd say I was pretty lucky compared to some.

The better I feel physically and the less self-absorbed, the more I'm beginning to think of others, particularly Jade who must be totally exhausted. Beautiful as ever, of course, but there's weariness in those large blue eyes. Much as it killed me to do it, I've told her not to come in so often, just three days a week instead of every day as she's been doing since my stroke. Of course, she argued with me at first, but I insisted. Four months is a long time to cope with all this emotional stress, and I'm worried. She needs her rest.

As for me, I spend the extra time working, an investment that's already paying dividends. I can now stand on my own! The other morning in physio, I pushed myself out of my chair with my good arm and stood up, firm as anything. Well imagine! Nobody behind me, nobody ready to grab a hold! I was laughing with pride and almost lost it. The bike, the endless pillow and foot-plate pushing, the hours of tensing = they've worked!

"Now you've no excuse!" says Alisha, a delighted smile betraying her no-nonsense tone, and she sets me up with sit-to-stand exercises from now on, working off the plinth with a table in front of me so I won't fall.

"Slave driver!" I joke, and again she smiles, knowing full well I whip myself harder than anyone else could. Already, I'm managing five to ten exercises in a session, making myself stand up until my knees start trembling with fatigue.

One area I haven't been happy with is my speech, which is why I rarely mention it, despite attending a meeting with David every day. That being said, I've managed to make some progress lately, thanks to a simple new device. "Let's try this," says David and before I can protest he plonks a nose clip on my hooter, the type that swimmers use. "Easy enough," I think, but it's bloody hard to get the hang of; I really struggle to coordinate my breathing, especially when I start laughing again.

David isn't deterred. "Don't worry, you'll soon get used to it. Just take it away and practice on your own."

So, I've been practicing – first with Jade and my family – and now, having finally got the hang of it, with the nurses. Okay, they need good hearing as my voice is very quiet but, if there's no background noise I can just about make myself understood. The problem is, what little air I have is escaping through my nose so my voice box is only operating at low volume. Never mind. It's just so great being able to connect again.

Still got the alphabet board (of course), which is now glued to my laptray for back up; although I'm trying not to use it as much, only as a last resort after two failed attempts at speaking.

Who'd have thought that a $7.50 nose clip, dangling proudly from my neck by a shoe lace, could so dramatically transform my life! In a matter of weeks, my alphabet board – my sole means of communication for three months – is virtually redundant. People can hear me! Amazed and delighted to have a voice again, I've started talking to the nurses, to the doctors, to the therapists, to the orderlies and cleaners - to anyone who'll listen. After getting the movement back in my arm, this is undoubtedly my next biggest turning point. It's wonderful being able to talk to my favourite nurses, to show my true personality at last. Before my stroke, I was nicknamed 'Ave-a-Chat', a name I'm rapidly reclaiming, even though my voice sounds ridiculous. But I don't care. As long as people listen carefully, they can understand me! If there's one thing I've missed, almost as much as feeding myself, it's been the ability to express myself.

And now, thanks to David and his brilliant, makeshift device, I can see light at the end of the tunnel - and stood in its radiant glow is Pete: Pete Coghlan with his off-the-cuff witticisms; Pete Coghlan making people laugh; Pete Coghlan chatting up the nurses; Pete Coghlan bantering with the guys; and best of all, Pete Coghlan telling Jade how much he loves her!

Naturally there's room for improvement, but day by day, I'm building up my vocabulary, sounding out words and repeating them until I can reel them off perfectly. David's assigned a student, named Courtney, to help me for a short time, encouraging me to join in group chats with other head-injury patients. To tell the truth, I find these sessions rather intimidating, as we all have speech issues; but Courtney is a lovely girl who makes me feel normal and, before long, I'm enjoying the experience. There are quizzes, competitions, girls versus lads, that sort of thing. Jade comes too sometimes and between us all, the sessions get pretty lively!

I'll be sad when Courtney leaves, just as one day I'm surely going to miss student nurses Judy, Sam and Ciara -

wonderful girls who, working in rota, have cared for me ever since my lifeless body was wheeled into Shenton. They've been so good, always knowing exactly what I need, and they even managed to make me laugh in those dark, early desperate days. I wish I'd known them all before my stroke and will certainly try to stay in touch. Whatever happens, they'll always be in my heart – just as I am in their debt forever!

I've started hanging around the toilets for the first time in my life, but this sudden urge to visit the loo in the evenings is due to the location of the only safety rail in the ward, which is helping me find my feet again. Once dinner's over and everybody else is tucked in for the night, I sneak inside, set up my iPod and use the rail to pull myself up, bending my knees slightly to stop them knocking. I've been doing this exercise for a few weeks and can now stand without holding on, keeping my hands hovering over the rail just in case. The nurses know what I'm doing and have so far left me to it. I've also told Alisha.

"Do you want me to change your mobility chart?" she said and, on seeing my smile of approval, wrote, "Independent in the bathroom" on the chart! This means I no longer have to wait for assistance whenever nature calls but can now visit the loo whenever I want to. All by myself. No more accidents. No more embarrassment. Bliss!

Emboldened by these massive strides forward, I've also been trying to reduce my medication – against the wishes of my doctors, I might add. I started by knocking off the anti-depressants, followed by Baclafen and tablets to keep my bowels loose, because I seemed to be spending most of my time just traipsing to the loo. Unfortunately, I'm now suffering from the reverse problem, which is proving highly embarrassing. For one thing, the end product is rather more difficult to dispose of than formerly. No matter how many times I flush, one of my stools is so enormous it clings defiantly to the bottom of the pan, impossible to budge. It takes several goes, me pumping the handle for all it's worth, and no doubt causing a drought, before the offending brown mass disappears like a giant torpedo to sabotage Perth's sewers.

There again, I should be thankful to pass anything at all! Another time I used the loo after stopping the tablets, an experience that makes me blush to this day! I was left alone to do my business, although there was a buzzer beside me just in case. Unfortunately, just like every other part of my body, my bowel and rectal muscles were weak, making it virtually impossible to push anything out.

Several minutes went by. Nothing! Another few minutes passed by. Still nothing! Gingerly, I started poking around with my finger, hoping this might trigger evacuation. At that precarious moment, just when things were beginning to 'happen', Clara, the staff nurse knocked on the bathroom door. "Need any help, Pete?" That was the last thing I needed! If I couldn't empty my bowels, the nurses would come swooping in, suppositories at the ready!

"Pete? Come on, you can't sit there all day!"

Her pleas were joined by one of my room-mates yelling: "Yea, come on, bro! There's a queue out here – get your finger out!"

Well, that did it! Struck by the hilarity of the situation, I burst into helpless, side-splitting laughter.

"Are you okay?" Asks Clara, now seriously concerned, no doubt mistaking my maniacal mirth for cries of anguish. Well, this just makes me laugh all the louder until I'm doubled up howling with hysteria at the thought of revealing my problem to her. Whatever these nurses get paid, it's not nearly enough!

Poor Clara, she has no choice but to throw me off the ward. I simply can't control myself, like a naughty school kid under the stern gaze of his headmaster, the more I try to stop, the worse it gets.

Mercifully, since that embarrassing incident, my muscles have started working more efficiently, so I've never had to 'go fishing' again!

Triggering any of my muscles into action is quite an art. To encourage a cough reflex, or to be sick "before my stroke", I used to tickle my epiglottis with my finger or something, a technique I tried 'now and again', much to Jade's consternation with my toothbrush! "Don't be an idiot, Pete!" she scolded. "You'll choke yourself doing that!" Despite her worries, I was determined to try, waiting until the nurses weren't looking to disappear into the bathroom, toothbrush at the ready. It didn't work now... In fact, with my weak arm, it was a dangerous, almost a suicidal thing to do. But that's me, always looking for ways to get myself right, never relaxing or keeping still. When I'm in bed, I practice lifting my legs, then my knees, determined to increase the level raised inch by painful inch, but because I see it, I want more! The obsession is now ruling every spare minute of my life. Even when I'm urinating, I stop the flow at least 4 times to strengthen my prostate.

"Build them up slowly," Alisha urges. "There's no need for pain." Well-meant as they are, her words go in one ear and out the other. Trouble with me, I'm too impatient; I've had enough of uselessness, of lying helpless in a hospital bed. So I keep exercising, going for the burn. I'll do whatever it takes, however long it takes, no matter how it hurts to get this stubborn body moving and get home!

In the meantime, Clara has forgiven me for my hysterical outburst. She's cool is Clara, always seeing the funny side. Other favourites are Kay, Charmaine, Anne-Marie, Genelle and Tash who I always look forward to seeing on the ward, as they'll always go out of their way for me whenever I need anything. In fact, all the nurses have been brilliant, male and female. When you're in hospital for months, you need the regular friendly faces, people you can rely on. The more I think about it, the more appreciative I am, and the more I realise I wouldn't be writing this if it wasn't for them. I might not remember every one by name, but I'll never forget what they've done for me, how they come to me at the start of their shifts to see if I need anything. How they spend a little time each day or night chatting to me and patiently listening to my still feeble voice. Never have I had to rely on anyone as much as I have on the staff at Chateau Shents. I will never forget them as long as I live. Never!

Chapter 13

The last month has literally flown by, thanks to all my rediscovered skills. I can now shower myself, although transferring from my wheelchair to the shower chair takes most of my strength. And, as long as I wear simple clothes such as shorts and T shirts, I can dress myself too. Socks are still a bit of a problem, owing to my right leg being way behind my left leg in agility. Undeterred, I've learned to lift my right leg over my left knee so I can do both feet, socks and trainers on – a big achievement from a nursing point of view, as I'm now virtually independent and, of course, a massive relief for me, even though the process is slow and often frustrating and you never see how far you change! (Something only strokies and ABIs would truly understand).

All I need now is my electric chair to get me about, which I hope won't be for much longer, because gradually, amazingly, incredibly, I'M LEARNING TO WALK AGAIN.

It's a precarious business at first, even though I only take one short step at a time. Yet I can always fall back on Alisha – literally! She walks behind me, her arms around my waist, bracing me as we promenade the length of the gym.

"What's this? Strictly Come Dancing?!" I quip.

"Yeah, and I'm Ginger Rogers!" Alisha replies. "Just keep walking, Pete!"

"Bet you say that to all the guys!"

"Nah, only cheeky ones like you!"

My tongue is improving now too, so much so that David has put me on to a soft food diet, expanding my menu to include some of my favourite dishes, such as boiled egg mashed in a cup – something my Nanna used to make me when I was a kid. Wow, it tastes so good with plenty of butter! I'm just disappointed that it's still hard to move any food around my mouth, as I really don't want to spit it out.

I've also been for a fluoroscopy – or swallow test - at Royal Perth Hospital. This is to see if I can take slightly thinner milkshakes or juice with my dinner without the liquid going down the wrong way. It's the second time I've been tested and, while realistically I don't expect much change, I'm quietly hoping for a miracle. First of all, the staff X-ray my neck then, starting with some thick, white liquid, they gradually introduce increasingly thinner variations to see how well I cope. I'm pleased to learn my swallow is much stronger, but I'm still not allowed water, which is gutting, as I'm desperate for a proper drink.

"Sorry, Pete," I'm told. "At this stage, it's just too dangerous."

Thank goodness for Brad. By way of compensation, he and Vicky bring me a Big Mac, drawing the curtains so I can scoff myself silly. I set to work, slurping down the food with a nice *thick*, strawberry milkshake and a great deal of gusto. The bread's a bit hard-going, but I devour the rest and burp happily!

My trusty brother-in-law is always cheering me up. Since I've become more independent, I'm on 'parole' at weekends, ready to make mischief and Brad has proved a willing accomplice, brimming with bright ideas, some too daft to mention. For instance, he accompanied me to our local bottle shop 2 or 3 kilometres away, just so he could film me wheeling in to the drive-through in my electric wheelchair – a clip which he later posted on You Tube.

"Everyone'll think I'm an alki!"

"You mean you're NOT?" says Brad. "Thought that's why you needed the chair!"

My electric chair has been customised with some really good specifications – including a (very loud) air horn thanks to Brad, which I use to great effect at Shenton Park. Armed and decibelled, I blast around the corridors, scaring the wits out of my chosen victims, especially the physio staff. One day they were sitting on the grass enjoying their lunch outside, taking in the sunshine without a care in the world - until I came screeching round the corner on 2 wheels, waiting for just the right moment to sound the horn, causing them all to jump with fright.

"Just wait 'til your next physio Pete! You'll wish you were back in the army when we've done with you!" they joke. At least I HOPE they're joking!

I've always tried to keep my sense of humour, even in those bleak, terrible days at the beginning of my illness. I had been in Shents for about two weeks, unable to move a muscle and I remember my OT saying something like "we need to get your brain sending signals to your hands, so what would you like to hold?" My Dad, Noi and Jade were there. I glanced at Jade and began to blink: "M-y d-i-c-k!" God only knows what the therapist thought, but my Dad creased up laughing. He and I share the same sense of humour.

Just as well. He has certainly needed it with me as a son, especially while I was in my teens. Once, when he and Mum were going on holiday, they made the mistake of leaving me in charge, no doubt believing that a bit of responsibility might encourage me to be, well, a bit more responsible. Perish the thought! While the parents were sunning themselves in blissful ignorance, all my mates were heading to the house, quickly followed by the rest of Whaley Bridge. The ever-growing mix of teenage girls, pimply lads, booze and music at full blast proved too much for the neighbours. Before long, the police were marching up the drive.

Now, I'm sure the officers were courteous enough to knock on their arrival; unfortunately, nobody could hear them above the thudding heavy metal.

Crash! The first I knew of their arrival was when the front door burst open and the invading riot squad brought the party to an abrupt end.

We got a right bollocking, of course, but worse than that was the horrible mess! One by one, guests disappeared, leaving me Dan and Matt to clear up behind them. "What are we going to do about the door?" said Dan. With me being a brickie and Dan doing a course in micro-electronics, we didn't know much about carpentry.

"We've got to do something!" I moaned, "My folks are due back tomorrow!"

Nine o'clock in the morning, we were at the Builders Merchants stocking up on plaster, wood and paint. Ok, I was used to cement, but plaster is another matter entirely. Even so, I reckon we did an outstanding job considering. Only thing was, it was too wet for us to paint over it, so we used my mum's hairdryer to help the plaster to set.

Mum and Dad arrived home as expected, took a brief look around the (now tidy) house and sighed with relief. Didn't they *trust* me or something? Anyway, I almost got away with it until the next evening when Dad went to close the Venetian blinds. Seconds later, he let out a roar. "Peter! Come here!" Sheepishly, I entered the room to see the rotting, half-eaten pizza, which had been breeding cultures behind one of the blinds, now scattered all over the sofa, oh and the discarded fag butt in the dainty en-suite sink! That pissed my mum off the most, I think, knowing people had been in her bedroom.

I'm sure Mum's forgiven me now – although to this day Dad doesn't know about the door! My old man's face, coppers at HIS door! Oh he was so mad with me!

Since my illness, he's been visiting me every couple of months, flying in and out from Thailand. One time he brought some much loved friends with him, who'd all clubbed together to buy me a fantastic new laptop to watch movies on and type my diary, which, I might add, has been great for getting my head back together. And Brad has bought me a Wi-Fi, so I can connect with the internet.

This has opened up a whole new world for me. Facebook is a great way to pass the time, to keep in contact with my friends Dan and Wes, Gav, Matt, Peter – everyone including family in the UK and Thailand. The irony is, I never touched computers before but, after ribbing Jade for her Facebook activities, things have taken a total flip and now I'M the social network freak!

It's certainly been the source of much encouragement, especially after I linked up with so many other survivors out there; that's given me so much hope. Jade still reads me inspirational stories but now I can search the internet myself, I've started to spend an hour a day typing my diary before my sleeping pills kicks in.

With so much going on, I haven't yet had time to miss my old friend John who was so encouraging to me during those first few weeks in Shenton. His departure was typically laid-back: "See you later, Pete!" he said, cheerily. "Look me up when you get out of here – we'll share a jar or two." I gave the thumbs up to that! "Of course, you'll have to get your right arm working properly first. Get yourself a glass of lager and keep raising it to your old mucker – good exercise, ey!" he grinned, earning another thumbs up from me.

Zoomer was eventually discharged but, sadly, barely made it home. My last memory of Zoomer was him pulling out a coffin nail, ready to light up before even reaching the exit. Swearing good-naturedly as the tut-tutting nurse pushing his chair, he waved his goodbyes to me and the others. Within weeks, we learned that he was dead. Whether it was the fags that killed him or he just ran out of puff, I'll never know. But I'll miss the cheeky beggar, even if he *did* nearly kill me - causing my infections because of laughing at his antics!

For the rest of us, life goes on and, I must say, it's great to be let out on leave so I can spend quality time with Jade. Last Sunday, 17th July, was my second outing and a truly memorable day. I was home for a whole six hours, lying bare-chested out in the sunshine trying to get some colour on my pasty skin! Lunch was good too - real potatoes, beans and (my favourite) boiled eggs mashed up in a cup.

Afterwards, I went to the park for the first time since my stroke, but that was definitely not as enjoyable. The 3 inch drop, off the concrete ramped curbs I was trying to negotiate, was pretty scary at first in my electric chair – a bit like taking a Go-Kart down a rollercoaster!

When I think of the hundreds of times I'd walked this route without ever giving it a thought. Now I know how hard the simplest trip can be for people in wheelchairs, I make a mental note to mention it to the relevant authorities.

Despite these difficulties, I enjoyed the sense of freedom of my short trip out – yet I fervently pray that next time I can walk it!

Chapter 14

Monday, 18th July 2011

Countless hours of mini squats are beginning to pay dividends. At last, I feel brave enough to transfer myself to bed unaided – an absolute no-no unless okayed on your chart, but then I'd never let other people's no-no's influence me much, not even in the army!

I pull the curtains shut around my bed then, slowly and carefully, stand from my wheelchair. Getting undressed isn't easy, as I have to stand up to pull my trousers down, then sit down so as not to fall. Shoes and socks can only be removed with the help of a special stick from OT, but I manage it, all by myself!

What a relief! The nurses haven't had to do anything for me this last week. I can feed myself, dress and undress myself, drive myself to therapy sessions and take myself for a shower, shave and, erm, the other business! The only thing I still need help with is my computer. Someone has to hand it to me once I'm in bed, as, being so weak, I'm afraid of dropping it. My laptop has become a vital piece of kit.

On top of all this, I'm gradually coming off my medication, all except for Aspirin! So it's all systems go ready for life after Chateau Shenton! Of course there'll be problems, like my speech for instance - how will people outside react to my strange, nasal delivery? But apart from such niggles, I'm thrilled at the prospect; I can't wait to be back with Jade, to lie on the sofa with my good arm around her. The thought of this is so warming; I'm determined to be as strong as I can to make life easier for her when I'm home.

So I've started a routine, a self-imposed fitness plan. Every night after therapy, I do five lengths of the corridor in my wheelchair, which isn't easy, as I can't grip the tyres properly so my fingers get trapped in the spokes now and then. This is followed by half an hour of squats against the bathroom door, a feat I can only achieve by keeping one hand on the handle (just in case).

Sometimes, I think I'm mad. Everybody else is in bed by 8 o'clock while I'm just getting going. Perhaps they want to chat to each other or their stroke wasn't as severe as mine, or maybe they're not as desperate as me. All I know is ... I want OUT. Out of Shenton, out of medication, out of uselessness, out of illness, and I'll do whatever it takes, even if it means becoming a body builder, anything to reverse my condition. I hate being so helpless; so weak, even the bedclothes are too heavy for me to lift. I never, ever, ever want to feel this way again.

Helplessness! Truth to tell, I spent a lot of my youth in just that very state – helpless from either booze or laughter or both! When I think back to boyhood, I sometimes wonder how I survived my teens, never mind the army and a concerted attempt by the IRA to send me packing to Kingdom come!

Back to the present battlefield! When not eating, sleeping, exercising or talking to Jade and my family, I think about everything that's happened since my stroke. Although the past few months are fairly muzzy, I can remember my feelings only too well - the pain, the panic, the sickening dread of the future. Being trapped in your own body is an experience I'd never wish on anyone else, not even my worst enemy. Which gets me thinking how self-absorbed I've been, obsessed with every fibre of my nervous system, with every feeble twitch, with every movement of my bowels. Now it's time to think of others, maybe write a book. If nothing else, I hope my experience will serve to help future locked-in survivors.

The more I think about it, the more I like the idea. Quite a challenge but it will give me a purpose when I get home. Nothing galvanises the brain more than a purpose. A body builder AND an author! Think I'll start keeping a diary.

Chapter 15

23rd July 2011

Good day today – managed to work up a sweat on the exercise bike, doing 9km in 32 minutes – shouts and cheers all round. "That's a record!" cries Alisha. Glad someone's keeping score! 9km, hey? Next time, I'll aim for 10!

I honestly believe that the stronger my legs get, the faster I'll go, the more efficient my lungs will become and the better my speech will be. In short, the longer I can go the louder I'll get – a daunting prospect for some!

When I first entered the gym, I felt my problems were a million times worse than anyone else's, but now I've realised there are people in here a lot worse off with less hope of full recovery. At least I'm starting at the bottom, advancing a little every day. But just as my speech, muscles, mobility and strength are being built up, people with degenerative diseases try to keep their muscles from atrophy - nice people who deserve better. It certainly makes me count my blessings.

There's one guy here, an officer with the Western Australian Police called Ryan Marron, a really fit, tough guy, who got locked-in after contracting Murray Valley Encephalitis from a mosquito bite! Just goes to show – you can follow the healthiest lifestyle ever, sensible food, no smoking or drinking, and be brought down by an insect you can barely see through a microscope! Poor Ryan is a twitching mess at the moment, although he'll probably get better faster than me. His wife seems nice; she and Jade have been out together a few times. I'm glad. It's good to bond with someone who knows what you're going through and I'm sure they'll become good friends.

Another positive, I've a really good feeling about my right arm. When Alisha manipulates it, the arm feels stronger, even though there's two of us moving it. I'm confident that moving my arm myself will soon be possible; just hope my fingers will benefit as a result.

Once that happens, I'll have to teach my brain to eat with my right hand again in order to build up its strength.

Amazing how heavy everything is; even though my left arm is working, it's hard work using the computer, as I have to press every key with one finger. I keep typing the wrong letters and have to delete every second word, but thank God I've one good arm, which is amazing, considering the doctors' original prognosis. They told my family I'd be paralysed from the head down – probably needing a high level of care for life. Imagine hearing that! Fortunately, they've been proved wrong and now they've seen it happen for me, I intend to make the rest of the world see just what can be achieved with determination.

I've had a big incentive, mind: Love. No matter what else happened, I just couldn't face losing my girl. What a jewel! Jade's been going through hell because of me, remaining stoically by my side, come what may. It must have been hard with her family living thousands of miles away. Friends have been supportive, but there are only so many depressing conversations her contemporaries can take!

At least she hasn't been totally alone. Dave's been there for her, watching over her, always ready to listen. To walk the dog, start the dinner, or just make sure the house is warm when she gets home. All the things I'd be doing but for this stroke, things I hope to do again one day.

Actually, I surprise myself at how 'responsible' I am these days, unlike the Pete of old. Sometimes, when I'm safely in bed at night, or doodling on my laptop, I smile to myself, my mind occasionally wandering to the follies of my youth. Misspent maybe, but boy it's been fun at times!

My partner in crime and childhood friend Dan Hodson was invariably involved somewhere along the line, despite his far from rebellious nature. All Dan really wanted to do was tinker with his car and stuff, but while I was on the scene he'd no chance of that. One night, after a few – actually, a LOT of drinks – me, Dan and two other mates, Wes and Matt, were staggering home from Marple when we chanced upon a rather comfy-looking sofa, conveniently placed on someone's front drive, no doubt intended for the refuse collectors.

"How considerate of them!" I exclaimed, "Fancy a sit-down, Dan?" This seemed as good a place as any to rest up, "Don't know about you lot, but I could do with a smoke." So we sat down and started chatting away.

"That wasn't very hospitable was it?" said Dan, referring to the landlord of the pub where we'd been drinking. "No," I agreed, "throwing buckets of cold water over us was not my idea of a good host!" we were leaving..."eventually"!

Dan grabbed the front of his shirt and squeezed the moisture out of it. "Well you did give him a mouthful of cheek, Pete! You can be a real arse at times!"

"Only at times? I must be slipping!"

Then Wes piped up. "I'm freezing!"

"So am I," said Matt, glaring at me reproachfully. By now it was after midnight so we were all feeling the chill. It then struck me as both practical and amusing to set fire to the sofa. Only problem was, Dan and the others were still sitting on it.

"Never mind," I said cheerfully, "I'll soon warm you up!"

My remark was met by moody silence and none of them noticed when I got my lighter out. Nor did they flinch when I torched the tassels which hung so temptingly from the back of the three-seater.

Much to my disappointment, the sofa didn't immediately burst into flames. Instead it began to smoke heavily.
"Arggh!" cried Wes looking suspiciously at his reefer. "What the...?"

He soon found out. The fire sprang enthusiastically to life and I collapsed into uncontrolled snorts of laughter watching my companions leap from the sofa. Matt's shirt tail started smoking, and Wes was there whacking his back.

"You idiot, Pete!" yelled Dan. "You could have roasted us alive man!"

At that moment, the bedroom light came on and the head of a furious man leaned out of the window.

"What the hell's going on down there, lads!?"

"Oh shit.. 'leg it lads!!!"

Pelting down the road at a spanking rate of knots, we headed back to Dan's house, the sound of fire engines sirens ringing in our ears. "Cogs, you Muppet!!!!!"

Funny at the time!..."Sorry lads."

23rd July 2011

I've just finished my breakfast not expecting very much out of the day, same-o same-o.... My right fingers still haven't opened, which is gutting – surely they should have improved by now! At least I can type. Think I'll write a few words today, starting with an email to Jade, to tell her how I feel about her. I do try to tell her when she's here but, with my vocals being so faint and weedy, it just doesn't sound the same. "I love you," in a weak Darth Vader voice hardly screams romantic hero 'ey'?

If only we could talk like we used to - Jade and me, the best of mates, just yack-yack-yacking for hours at a time; but at the moment, I just can't speak quickly enough – I run out of breath support before I can say what I really want, relying on my listener's patience. Also, my voice is still so soft I can't pronounce the words clearly, they can scarcely be heard. I feel pathetic.

"One day at a time!" they all say. All very well, but it's painfully slow, like waiting for grass to grow! No, actually, it's worse – more like waiting for a tree, a huge oak tree!

Must count my blessings; my legs are working, my back's okay, I can use one arm to eat now, also my stomach muscles are engaging a little more. Judy was right too! Being upright in my wheelchair HAS strengthened my core, but nothing strong enough yet! I just dream of sitting up by myself again some day but my right arm is "still" not able to even lift the damn covers off my bed! I try not to worry about it, telling myself "it'll come", "it'll come"! The truth is I really don't know.

Please God, let me get better. Jade needs me!

The most important thing to me is to GET HOME!! Once there, I can learn to talk properly again which will hopefully not take long. Realistically, I'll will have to keep training for years to get back to how I used to be – a whole lifetime, maybe!

Life, hey! One minute I was planning to work for myself and now the best I can hope for is to get out of here someday. If that happens, I really don't care what I do, just as long as I can live at home and hug my wife. Adversity puts things in perspective big time. My days used to be one big rush; now I'm waiting, waiting, waiting, greedily grabbing almost every minute of the day to lift my legs or any part of me that'll budge in the hope of speeding things up. And it's working, I think, but you can hardly see the changes. Mum says she can!

Jade's a bit later than usual; she went to our friend Julia's birthday yesterday, "Bet she's hung over." If there's one good thing to come out of this illness, it's that I'm determined to keep my drinking down. And, of course, I no longer smoke, nor will I ever do anything to risk ending up in a hospital again. In fact, the thought of getting old in one is totally hellish! Having converted to the no-smoking brigade, I've become a right bloody preacher! I'm trying to persuade Jade to kick the habit too. I simply couldn't bear to see her go through any pain, not ever!

As the sun begins to sink, I indulge in an hour of grim reflection in the gardens outside Ward 7, re-living those horrific first days after my stroke. Before I get too immersed in these horrible memories, Jade appears, but somethings wrong. She's sobbing!

"I've just had an accident!" she wails. "Someone smashed into the back of me in the car park!"

Good job we're insured. "Don't worry. It's only a car Jade." I wanted to give her a big hug and I was more upset that I couldn't properly! I can hardly believe my attitude – at one time I'd have been bouncing with rage! Now, it's just one more hassle we could do without, scarcely worth a shrug. Besides, our luck's got to change sometime! Surely?

Chapter 16

25th July 2011

There are three new residents in my room: Keith, a man in his 60s, Peter who's in his 40s and Ryan Marron, (mentioned previously) who was infected by a mosquito bite. He was working up north at the time, in the wilds of Halls Creek, and had to be ferried to hospital with the Flying Doctor Service. At the moment, things don't look good for him. His bowels are all over the place and he has an intravenous peg for fluids, poor guy. He's only 29 – even younger than me.

Peter suffered a one-sided stroke and doesn't seem that bothered about it. In fact, he's a real wag, bringing a much-needed sense of fun into the ward; something which has been sadly lacking since Zoomer left. Don't reckon it'll be long before Peter leaves though – back to his farm in Geraldton to wait for his left side to come back.

I've just finished dinner. I think I've inhaled some pear. God I hope not – more antibiotics are the last thing I need right now and I'm a bit down at the moment.

Latest news on the ward... Amy Winehouse was found dead in her flat this morning! Can't say I was a big fan, but it's big news in the music world.

Anyway, time for my leg lifts....

Yay! Great physio session! I managed 13km on the bike then stood for a whole 5 minutes on my own.

I also keep trying as hard as I can to push my arm in the air, but can only manage a third of the way. That's disappointing as I really pushed hard today as well; getting used to it now.
Tomorrow...tomorrow....tomorrow!

My standing transfer is going ok – at least I've not fallen yet. I don't trust my dodgy leg. If only it was as strong as the other one I'd be flying on that bike. Never mind 13km – I'd be going for the ton!

Encouraged by my physical progress, I decide to

tackle the doctor about my anti-depressant tablets, telling him I want to stop taking them. "Okay," he says, "but you need to come off them gradually Pete! We'll drop the dose to 75mg." As he seems fairly amenable, I try to beat him down a milligram or two. "Tell you what", I bargain, "make it 50 and you're on!" He laughs. "How could I resist! 50mg it is, then!"

All in all, a positive day, despite my being more knackered than usual. I had to have a second Temazepam last night because Ryan was moaning constantly. My guess is he believes that by continually using his voice he'll get out of here quicker. Guess I was the same in the beginning! When I had a single room, I'd stay up all night trying to sound out "I... love... you" and" How... are... you" and "hello" over and over again. I didn't realise my soft pallet wasn't working. What a nightmare! Thanks to my "swimmer's nose clip" things have improved dramatically.

Occupational therapy next; "bloody hell!" It's my least favourite therapy – not because of the staff but because I never seem to learn anything, unless you can count getting more proficient with an electric chair. That sounds terrible ey? "I JUST WANT MORE PHYSIO" That'll get me home quicker I reckon! At least they have stopped them damn OT shower checks – felt so undignified!

Okay, back ward-side. I'm sitting here bursting for the toilet, waiting for a nurse to help. Unfortunately, it's a busy night; one patient has already messed himself and the nurses are cleaning him up. Ben and Steve are on duty tonight, so I'm not as worried. I try not to bug them too much unless I really need help. I see nurses struggling to keep up with the call bells, some times 3 bells go off at the same time and they struggle to get to everyone.

And now the bloody Internet's acting up! For most of my adult life I've avoided computers and I'm now totally dependent on videos, email and writing my diary – the only way I can communicate my thoughts coherently.

I met a guy called Tim today, a student physio who worked with me in the pool. He seems fine. More importantly, he's been helping me get my bad arm moving, using floating dumbbells to push it under the water in a circular forward motion, which puts pressure on my triceps. I belive in this movement, and just can't wait for more hydrotherapy sessions!

Chapter 17

26th July 2011

Speech with David and I'm so embarrassed! Half-way through the session I burst out crying. Whether it was due to sheer frustration or the drop in my anti-depressants, I don't know, but I'm not telling the doctor in case he ups the dose again. I'm determined to give 'em' up. Apparently, the long term effects can be 'TOTAL' dependency! Jade was on them for a while and found it really hard to come off them - they're extremely addictive.

On a lighter note, I'm watching a program called "An Idiot Abroad." He's so funny! Just like my mate Gav. "DOING ME E'D IN THIS!" is his favourite saying. Mine too!! Leaves me in stitches.

Now my bowels start rumbling....least I don't need to ring the bell anymore!

27th July 2011

I'm buzzing today! A nurse who's been on vacation for 10 days watches me open-mouthed.

"I can't believe how you've changed, Pete!" she exclaims. "And you're talking louder too!"

"Don't encourage him!" Craig says.

I suppose I have improved over the past week or two. I can now formulate words, albeit quietly, and am no longer using the alphabet board. Hope my voice gets louder before Christmas. Some of my friends are coming from the UK and it'd be awsome to talk to them properly. That nurse filled me with so much positivity! Fuelled me big time!

I've just done a massive 20km on the recumbent bike, amazing what the right words can do ey!

30th July 2011

Showered and ready for breakfast. While able to wash more and more of my body, showering is hard. I can just about reach my arse but find reaching my head rather more challenging. I only manage three-quarters altogether, because my arm gets heavy and I daren't risk doing my feet in case the commode tips up, so I have to leave them for the nurses.

Jade has just texted me to say she's on her way with the hair clippers. She always gives me a Number 2 - shaving my head all over; I'm surprised I have any at all after the shock of being locked in!!

At physio, I discover I can get to a sitting position myself. I started laughing uncontrollably with a look of triumph at Alisha. See Pete! 'Just keep cracking eggs'!

She tried some electrodes too on my feet! It stimulates the muscles and prevents the joints stagnating, I think she said?

The Ward is trying me on fish at the moment, "Awsome"! So far so good, but I have to be watched for my own safety. It's irritating!!! Nonetheless, chewing slowly and very, very carefully I manage. Sometimes it takes me half an hour or more to make the flesh soft enough to swallow!

David (supervising me) is very understanding and more like friend than therapist, so I really look forward seeing him. In fact, I can't fault anyone here really in Shenton Park, they've all been brilliant. When I'm travelling around in my chair, everyone says "Hello", as if I was famous or something - either that or they all feel sorry for me, not sure which?

I saw my old physiotherapist Leanne yesterday, who popped in while I was on the exercise bike. This time I achieved my 21st kilometre, just as she entered the gym.

I knew she'd go back and tell every one at Sir Charles Gairdner G51, who fed and cleaned me. They will now know I'm on the mend, and I don't mess the bed anymore!!!

A bit of dignity back in my mind I guess!

Back in my room, one of the nurses has just been confiding in me regarding her love life. It's so good to hear normal talk, when people talk to you as though you are human being - a real person whose opinion they value! Something I think I'd forgotten.

2nd August 2011

Alisha came up with a cool idea to get my arm going better today, involving a walking stick of all things! Amazing how, with all our modern technology, it's often the simplest aids that prove effective. The big news in Shents is my new roomies have arrived. One of them is an absolute nightmare; he has a guard with him all night with whom he argues constantly! At 2.30am, he demands a cup of tea, complains, says he has missed half the day and tries to get out of bed. When the guard told him to stay put, he told him to 'f*** off' - and loudly too, with none of the charm shown by Zoomer. As with Zoomer, though, the staff always knew when he's set for a wander! This guy screams loudly every time he gets up, which is bloody annoying for the rest of us!

Next morning, I'm awoken to his dulcet tones: "I need a shit.... Quick!!!! I'm going to mess myself!" No manners, no "Please" or "Thank you" for the nurses, and it's hardly what I need to hear first thing in the morning. Adding insult to injury, the guy not only shouts, but he has a mat at the side of his bed that squawks like a strangled canary whenever he steps on it – to let everyone know he's escaping! It's an awful sound that goes straight through me.

The other guy is okay, except for his annoying cough. Every four seconds it's cough,... cough,... cough, which is driving me mad, and he's only been here a day! I raised the matter with Bev, the head nurse, hoping to be moved to Ward 10 (also known as the 'departure lounge'), but it's out of their hands due to a lack of beds.

That ticks me off; when they want me to get better, but won't let me sleep in the quiet environment that I so badly need!

"Hope he behaves himself tonight"!

4th August 2011

This may not sound much to anybody else but yesterday I touched my nose for the first time - with my RIGHT hand. And today, I opened my first fruit purée, stripping the lid all the way off with my left fingers! Normally I have to use my teeth.

Yet these small achievements pale in comparison with my physio session today. Having managed an impressive few kilometres on the bike recently, today I decide to go for the burn.

Hauling myself onto the seat, I start peddling. Not much resistance, just enough to burn! 20km and 40 mins later I'm still going... Today my months of focus, anger and many days of tears came together!

"Easy does it," Alisha advises. "You're not in a race."

Yes I am. A race to get home!

"Twenty-one kilometres!"

Aware that something momentous is happening, everyone in physio starts looking over. One by one, they start cheering me on as the pedometer keeps whirring and my legs keep turning.

"Twenty-two kilometres!"

"Go for it!" yells one of the guys, his encouragement echoed by the rest of the gym.

"Twenty-five kilometres...!" cries Alisha.

The whole of the gym is yelling encouragement.

"Keep going Pete!"

"You can do it!"

"Twenty-seven kilometres...!"

"It must be a record!"

But I'm not finished yet....

"Thirty kilometres!!!!" yells Physio Pete. I felt absolutely euphoric! The staff and my fellow patients start cheering.

"Yay! Good on yer Pete! Whoowhooo!"

Alisha helps me transfer back into my chair. I'm exhausted, but very, very chuffed with my self. That day something was born inside me! I believed more than I ever did in my recovery. Nobody was stopping me! I wanted MORE!.... "I was going home, damn it!"

News of my record-breaking bike ride spreads quickly. I'm hardly back on the ward before Craig comes over to congratulate me.

"Heard about your exploit in the gym today!" he says. "You're doing really well, Mate. Keep it up."

Despite his smile, I detect a trace of sadness behind it.

"What's up, Mate?" I ask. Craig has become a really great mate, Talking with me whenever he can, listening patiently to my nasally speech, and sharing my tears when I get low. Now it's my turn to lend a sympathetic ear.

"I've just come from OT," he says.

"And....?" I prompt.

He pauses for a moment, trying to maintain composure. "Seems I'm stuck...told me I might not get the movement back in my arms..." Craig's down big time. Don't people realise how words can destroy us in seconds?

"Hope is all we have"!

Looking at my destroyed mate I said, "Take no notice of them, Craig! That's exactly what they told me not so long ago. And now look..." I lifted my left arm to demonstrate my point. Why, I could even wrestle a crocodile with my left arm! Well, a newt, maybe!"

Craig smiles. "Yes, things seem to be working out for you, don't they?"

"And I was a lot worse than you when I first came in. A lot worse!"

"*Don't* be afraid – use it as fuel," I tell him. "Don't let them grind you down. You'll get your arms going again mate!"

Craig smiles again, encouraged I hope. If anyone deserves a break it's him. Just wish, deep down, I could be as sure of our recoveries.

Chapter 18

Back at the ward, the staff have found a solution to the nutter in the opposite bed. They take him down to the TV room at 9.30pm, providing me with a few hours of bliss. I'm sleeping so much better now, thank God.

And how I need it after all that exercise! I feel like I've just run a marathon, but I'll never be satisfied now, I know this because I feel my hunger growing! For hours on end, I move my body in weird, stupid ways - rocking Alisha's walking stick back and fourth, holding my legs out in front of my wheel chair, or moving my tongue like a snake in my mirror for hours.

It's all paying off though; finally, I'm being allowed home tomorrow for a "whole" night! I can't believe it. This is the biggest thrill. Jade says she's going to cook shepherd's pie for dinner - home cooking at last! I am sooo looking forward to sleeping in my own bed, holding Jade as best I can, but I'm worried about having no safety rail so I don't roll over the side! "Jade will stop me failing".

I'm sure it will be fine, though - I'm certainly not going to lose any sleep tonight. Early to bed, ready for a good start. Trust me, when that maxi taxi arrives at nine, 'I'll be ready'! Craig and Kelly are coming too, as they live close by, which is reassuring. Although I've been home before, it's always been with Jade; this will be the first day I'll travel without her.

Being out in public scares me, and I am embarrassed to say that, but bad speech and being in a wheelchair gives me anxiety! What ifs...

What if suddenty I need to go?

What if my wheelchair breaks down?

As it happens my weekend was ok I guess!

Jade tried her best to make me laugh, it was funny when she had to inject my stomach with my home meds; she hated that bit, me giggling like a child! She hates the way I drop to the age of 5 years old in a second, "just no emotional control at all!"

Being home isn't the same now; I got stuck too, bogged right down in Perth's sandy grass! Swear my house was once on the sea bed! I find shells in my soil, being 5km away from a beach I guess we were once. Very flat here, hope we never get a tsunami; I can't swim now, stupid thought, as if I could swim would help! I find myself playing out my vulnerability – stop this right now Pete!

Hate watching Dave, Jade, and Cody watch me leave. As I get loaded by ramp in the Maxi taxi I get quite emotional; that's when I think most about the memories, the person I was. I look at my boat not covered properly. I want to shout out to Dave as the lift takes me up, but he'll never hear me! Its only a boat I try to remind myself.

The driver straps me in and bolts me to the taxi floor, and I wave, 'trying to be brave'.

The guy opposite is asleep. Wish he learned to sleep when we do, the d***head. And he smells the place out! But what really gets my goat is his rudeness to the nurses – never says 'please' or 'thank you', just gives them a load of abuse! That's another reason why I think they should be paid more; nurses deserve better. Much better.

They always put their patients before their well needed breaks, even when they need the loo themselves! Some people just treat them like crap, gets me really mad!

10th August 2011

Today I'm working on my right leg using a 'Pilates Reformer' which seems to be working, as I can feel my leg burning. It's simple really; I lie down on a sliding platform and push with my feet. As the body moves, it slides away leaving the legs to take the strain, "good piece of kit I reckon."

Mum has just left after helping me sort out my drawers. The nutter across the way has been taken out of the room for now, because he has Golden Staph – or, to give it its posh name, Staphylococcus Aureus – a bacterium that lives on the skin or in the nose. Common enough and normally harmless, the bug can cause a range of infections from mild to severe, yet some strains are resistant to antibiotics, and can even prove fatal for vulnerable hospital patients with surgical or other wounds. It's also highly contagious, and any trace of it means double the usual work for cleaners. Getting rid of the germs involves scouring every inch of the ward, and everything has to be moved into the corridor, including draws, cupboards and all personal belongings. It was a right mess and it cocked everyone's day up. All the nurses were grouchy and just wanted to go home, so no one has put anything back and we're having our dinner in the TV room – arriving just in time for the news.

England's having riots in every major city including Manchester and Salford. Don't know what's caused them, and I normally don't watch the news much because there's too much to be done – exercising or writing my diary.

11ᵗʰ August 2011

Back to school, sitting in the education room with no Thai book, so they kindly let me write my diary instead. The staff seem nice, everyone seems nice - the secret is to keep smiling and everyone remembers you, I reckon it helps anyway!

Today in physio Alisha was at a meeting, allowing me to stay on the tilt table longer; 'supervised', doing half sit-ups to my heart's content. I lost count of how many, but I did as many as I could, stopping to stretch my calves and then carrying on... I'm determined to do a full sit-up by the end of the month if it kills me! I hate having to be lifted up by others, especially by pregnant nurses!

Occupational therapists are coming back to my house tomorrow to see what I will need – that's the side of OT I like! Best tell them I'll definitely need a spar ey! Ha-ha. They're going to put a bench in the shower for me to make it safe and maybe lend me a rail for over the bed, so I can pull myself up and to help me to roll over.

14th August 2011

This weekend, I've been given two days home leave, so we've been to lunch with our friends Julia and Sean. Julia made a rice dish that was great, but I had to take my time as it wasn't very moist and l struggled a little. All the while I was there I was desperate to get out my bloody chair and sit like everyone else round the table - commonly named the 'Volvo' as it's sturdy.

They put a box under my feet to stop my right leg swelling up as it tends to do recently, goes really blue! I was also dying to get in the spa like we used to. Oh, how I miss the old days! I'll never forget sitting in the spa one summer during a lightning storm, no rain, just flashes across the sky. Australia can put on a right display in summer, me smoking Ganja in one hand, holding a double scotch in the other, thought I was "living the dream!" I was in there for hours. "Felt like Al pacino in Scarface."

Now I realise the dream is just being able to hold things, full stop!

Nice though it is to be home, I can't stop thinking about getting myself right; always in the back of my mind. I'm saying "Must fix myself, I must fix myself," because being home is a big reminder of all the things I want to be able to do again. The two things I miss the most is walking and talking effortlessly. I sometimes wish I could spend every day in the gym, the only time I feel I'm making progress. Knowing I am in there keeps me mentally stable I feel. I'm so sick of this situation; I just want it to be over. When I get out of this wheelchair, I'll walk every day - just wait and see! I'll do whatever it takes...

Jade bought me a Wii game console which will be good therapy for my hands. Firstly, I enjoyed watching my sister Vicky and her husband, Brad, try the boxing game. It was really funny – and they were totally knackered after two rounds of punching fresh air. I think I'll get a lot of good use out of it "when" I get home.

Chapter 19

30th August 2011

Having been told I've only a month left in Shents, I am getting cocky, I guess because I'm in the doghouse! I took myself to the shower this morning, earning myself a good ticking off. "I'll be alright with the bars there," I reason, but I can see by the nurse's face she's not happy. "Don't you realise, if you slipped you'd not only put yourself back six months, but we'd have loads of paperwork to complete. And frankly, we've better things to do Pete!"

I suppose she has a point and I apologise. I just enjoy the luxury of going to the toilet whenever I want. NO shower just yet! At least my physio is sympathetic. Alisha's going to change my status today to 'Independent in the bathroom', which should give me a lot more freedom. I can also get into bed now by myself.

On my way to speech therapy, I'm thinking how to ask David if I can stop going in favour of physio, as I want to concentrate on building up my physical strength to make it easier on Jade when I get home. Although speech is very important to me, I don't expect much to change over the next month and besides, I can talk well enough to be understood. It's really a matter of breath control and my soft pallet and lungs need work, physio I 'think' will give me that! Hope David will be cool about it.

There's certainly a lot to organise and we're having a meeting to discuss my needs when I get home. I plan to acquire an exercise bike which will enable me to exercise even harder! At least it'll be my own environment from now on; my own garden with its little vegetable patch and endless planting to be done! Though I say it myself, I've green fingers (when they're working), and I may even make a bit of money by selling the cuttings from my garage once a month, perhaps help towards the shopping. Hard to believe, not long ago I was earning a thousand dollars a week; now I'll be lucky to make 50 a month!

After beating cancer, I returned to bricklaying where I became very competent doing extensions, knocking through conservatories, building garden walls – an all-round good brickie! Not this time. Don't think I would make much money laying bricks from my electric throne!

"What am I going to do now!"

I did my first car transfer today. It was hard as we have a 4x4 but I managed it, OT supervised my achievement, this was a big tick for my release!

2nd September 2011

Friday afternoon, rainy and cold, and I'm sitting in the café on my own, fed up because I was looking forward to mowing the lawn, or at least trying to, by pushing it with my electric chair. Oh well there's a whole summer on its way and I'll be at home soon enough, thank God, although I'll miss Shenton Park slightly. After five months, you kind of get used to everything, and everyone gets used to you.

The cleaners, cooks, library staff, security "Don't go home. We'll miss you here Pete."

To tell you the truth I was scared of leaving!

"My safety bubble."

Chapter 20

Unbelievably, a family meeting was called to discuss my possible discharge today. Mum, Jade, Vicky and my friend Dave are all here for this momentous occasion. David, Alisha, Bev (Ward Coordinator), my social worker and the occupational therapy team are here too, all saying positive things to support the idea.

"So when can I leave?" I ask. Christmas I knew was the original date put forward.

"Well," says Alisha, "Would 2 weeks time be soon enough?" She looks round at the others who smile approvingly. That's three months earlier than originally suggested – just six months and a day after being pole-axed by my stroke. Before I know it, the meeting is over.

"There'll be one more meeting before you leave," says the staff nurse, "just to discuss home help if needed. "But we won't be rid of you entirely," Alisha adds. "You'll still be coming in here as an outpatient."

I can hardly believe it! To go from having nothing but a pair of eyes that can only look up and down, to being considered fit enough for home! Of course, I'd still go to outpatients most days and for speech therapy as well – but I still can't believe it. Seems there's light at the end of the tunnel at last. Thank God I wasn't stuck in the early stages. I'm not a hundred percent sure my recovery was all down to me, but I like to think it was; night after night thinking of crab claws, trying to touch finger to thumb and finally being rewarded one morning when my thumb twitched a millimetre; I haven't quite understood what I did either. Thinking about the movement 'must' reconnect nerve fibres?

For my last few weeks here in Shenton, I ask David if I can eat a normal diet. At first he looks dubious but finally relents... "Well, o-kay," he said, "but order with caution!" Of course I will! Vindaloo's first on the list! Seriously, though, I'm thrilled. Everyone else gets to pick their own meals – "finally" now so can I, after five months of pap! Just as well I can use my hand to tick the menu boxes. It's great choosing breakfast – my usual was three bowls of porridge, but this week –"bacon"! It never tasted better!

Other treats new to me – takeaway Pizza "WOW"... Hard work bread, but I was in heaven for that moment!

On visits to the café, Craig bought me my first Mrs Macs pie! Craig's been really good to me and we've spent a lot of time together, becoming lifelong friends for sure. We sit on the grass, me with my pie and Craig with his coffee, chatting about our hopes and plans for the future.

Craig's leaving Shenton about the same time as me. Although, to me at least, Shenton Park seemed the most miserable place on earth when I arrived, we agree we'll miss it – especially the people who work here. A bit like leaving school; overwhelming joy, sprinkled with sadness.

I'm spending much of my time taking photographs on my cell phone at the moment – with a view to a possible book. At the very least, I want to publish my experience in some form to help others who find themselves locked-in as I was. No one else could quite comprehend the fear that locked-in survivors undergo, nor could words or pictures ever convey the sheer horror of the situation. That's why I'm now determined to provide as much encouragement and guidance as I can for fellow sufferers.

Speaking of encouragement, I think of all the people here who have been so brilliant and wonder how I'm ever going to say 'goodbye'. Jade has made gift baskets of chocolates and wine for all the staff, including regular nurses and therapists, but we will have these delivered after my departure, knowing I just can't cope with prolonged farewells. A few exceptions – my regular nurses and therapists, especially Alisha, whom I want to thank personally. Along with Craig, these are the people I shall miss the most.

There's also been a lot of packing to do. All my possessions have been packed and stored in neat piles around my bed for several days, much to everyone's amusement - but I can't help it. Like a kid on Christmas Eve, I'm so excited I can scarcely sleep and am sitting up writing my diary into the small hours.

"Looking forward to home?" says my night nurse Anne-Marie. I smile up at her, trying not to look too pleased at the prospect. But she understands; she and the rest of the staff are genuinely delighted for me.

"You know, we thought you'd be here for a good while longer – yet here you are, able to stand on your own two feet. No one expected that you know; not for another 6 months at least. In fact..." she pauses, mentally calculating my progress, "it probably IS a record in Shenton Park! I'll check that out!"

"Really!" "Awesome!" Seems like tensing and pillow pushing and all those squats have paid off big time! So glad I kept trying, ey Anne-Marie! I will miss you... I start welling up!

"Aw, you'll always be in our hearts, Pete! Now try and get some sleep or you won't be going anywhere!"

Chapter 21

Finally, it's the Big Day. Four o'clock in the afternoon. I'm fully packed, showered, dressed, powdered and perfumed with Cerruti 1881 aftershave. I may not feel so dashing at present, but WOW, I smell smooth!

Ready, correct and raring to go! But first, the hard bit. Jade wheels me out of Ward 7 and we head for the gym; the haven of hope which I've been visiting twice a day since my arrival at Shents.

With a loud blast of my fog-horn I summon everyone's attention, as I enter for the last time as an in-patient. Startled, everyone turns to look, including Alisha and Craig.

"Can I have a picture?" I ask. Alisha agrees and stops teaching for a couple of minutes to pose with me.

I was dying to show Alisha the banner that my friend Sue Bathols had organised for me as part of the leaving celebration. Little did I know, until they unrolled it, the great lengths that Sue had gone to create a wonderful, four foot "No longer Locked-in" banner; she had even colour coded the letters to match the yellow, red, blue, pink, grey, orange and green of my alphabet board. What a truly special gift.

"Here Alisha!" I say gruffly and hand her the basket of wine and chocolates. "Thanks, Peter," she says and bends down to hug me. "I'll really miss you, I will."

"Lucky day for me I got you as my physio..." I say, "...you're obviously an expert with locked-in syndrome."

"Expert? Me?" Alisha exclaims with a short laugh. "No way – you were my *first*! My first ever locked-in patient."

I start back with surprise. "That means I was your Number 1 ey!"

"Aw, you'll *always* be my Number 1, Pete! I don't think I've ever come across anyone in my life as determined as you!"

Feeling the tears welling up, I turn away so Alisha can't see them, only to lock eyes with Craig who's already crying unashamedly. Fat lot of help HE is in controlling my emotions. Nevertheless, I manage to wave cheerily enough, although my heart was close to breaking at having to say 'goodbye' to him and to Alisha and everyone. Craig can only just speak himself, choked he is with emotion.

"See you around, Mate!"

I take one last look around the gym, then swivel my chair towards the exit, trying to get through it as fast as I can before the situation becomes unbearable. Just as well my other therapists, David and Joslyn, were at a meeting in Perth, so sparing me even more heartache.

Mum, Ted, Vicky and Brad are waiting by reception as Jade wheels me into a side room and help me get ready for the great WALK OUT. For this, I've chosen my outfit carefully - a smart polo shirt, jeans and a rather fetching baseball cap. Jade considers my appearance, giving me the once over to ensure I'm looking my best.

"Will I do?" I ask.

"Hmmm, there's something missing," Jade replies. Lovingly, she uncoils my gold chains and places them around my neck. They feel good against my skin after so many months when my only adornment was a PICC line.

"Thank goodness for that Jade!"

"Pete Coghlan, are you ready?"

Vicky and Brad, from their vantage point in the corridor, have already set their video cameras whirring – one camera each, just in case!

"Shall we go?" says Jade.

I nod. No more goodbyes, no more to be said. I pause and take a deep breath, determined to keep a straight face, but a lump in my throat! Walking out of here with my head held high, with dignity and pride was so important to me! For a fraction of a second, the nerves kick in and I begin to quiver but - encouraged by a radiant smile from Jade - slowly, carefully, deliberately, I uncurl myself from my chair and hold myself erect. My regiment would have been proud of me today!

What a sight awaits me. It seems everyone in the unit knew the time of my discharge and is standing in the corridor, forming a line of honour. Afraid of falling, I grasp Jade's hand to steady me in case I make a prat of myself. But I needn't have worried. Concentrating hard, I focus on my destination, the exit to which Jade and I progress step by careful step. My right leg is over-extending and a little painful and there's a bit of a wobble but, cheered on by the nurses and my family and the thought of cameras, nothing is going to stop me; not now, not knowing how much I'd endured for this day to happen. I also owe it to everyone who has ever suffered locked-in syndrome; to show them they can do it too!

At last we reach the exit, me still upright, Jade's hand still in mine, and together, for the first time in months, we walk out into the sunshine.

It would be nice to end the scene there, all romantic and epic and all that. But with my sense of humour, I can't resist one last wind-up – me acting up for the camera*, doing doughnuts in my wheelchair, fog-horn blasting, tearing up and down outside the main entrance. If I hadn't been discharged already, I'd no doubt get evicted from the premises for sheer hooliganism. I just hope it gives everyone a laugh.

"Hurry up!" says Jade, "The taxi's here!" Sure enough, the Maxi cab rolls up to take Jade, me and my electric chair, while the rest of the gang travel separately. "Race you back home!" I shout. "Last one back gets the first round in!"

And it's over.

I'm free.

(Above) Norman holding Noi with Jade and Eileen (In honour of Norman's death a few years after this photo) at Shenton Park.

(Right) Jade and me at Shenton Park, 3 months in.

(Below) Me with my mum (Anne), sister (Vicky) and Alisha at Alisha's gym - my last day, leaving Shenton Park.

(Above) Returning home, start of reborn.

(Left) 16km walk in Perth city with Professor Blacker

(Below) Me, today, in the pool with my nephew, Jett.

Perth city

IN THE BLINK OF AN EYE – REBORN

I was asked by many survivors, from various parts of the world, if I would write about my life after walking proudly off my ward.

In the Blink of an Eye – Reborn is the rest of my story, told with complete honesty.

Peter Coghlan ☺

Chapter 22

I was so happy to get my dignity back, to be home again! But being home was a shock. I was pleased, of course, but nothing was the same now! Not sure Jade was quite as pleased as me, either. I don't know if she ever got used to my spasms in the night, nor the odd elbowing in the face as I turned over. It was still hard for me, and her face too!

To tell you the truth it hit me hard. I cried, looking at my garden; it had all turned to rat shit! I had so many memories, summers on my knees building stone walls, the pizza oven, block paving and plants - well don't get me started there - the trips to the garden centre, all the digging planting, etc. We always made it beautiful, that's for sure, but the garden was the last thing on Jade's mind this last 6 months.

I still had to use a rail for turning over; the shape of it was a bit like those you see in a passageway to stop motor bikes, but bent under the mattress then hovered at the side of the bed. But since I didn't really have any stomach muscles it was still a plus.

I lay awake most nights with insomnia, but I wasn't bothered. At first as I was so grateful to be home; the sound of her breathing next to me was something I remember clearly to this day! I just lay there thanking God for normality, no more buzzing in the corridor from the call bells of all the other patients, or angry shouting from the odd strokie who needed guards to control them! That used to frighten me! I was so vulnerable! I couldn't believe this had been my last 6 months, was it even real?! I didn't know what the days ahead had instore for me, but I had to believe I could get better than I was.

Jade was worried about going back to work after spending a month at home with me. She didn't want to leave me on my own. I promised to stay in my electric chair until she returned home from work, 'she didn't like that much either', well... the flack I got! "YOU MUST HAVE AN ALARM, WHAT IF SOMETHING GOES WRONG?"

I didn't want a care alarm. Two reasons: 1) I didn't want the $500 extra expense for Jade, and 2) because I knew older people had them. Crazy, ey??? Well, I didn't see how stupid that was back then, I was one stubborn fool for sure!

Then mum was on my case. "YOU MUST HAVE A CARE ALARM PETER YOU BLOODY IDIOT!!! Mum had worked in all areas of care from palliative to all care in the community, both in the UK and here in Perth. So she was less than impressed with my refusal ha-ha. But they were not getting through to me, so they let me be, respecting my wishes. True to my word, day after day I stayed in my chair, using a pee bottle still to be safe.

Those first months, I just enjoyed not being monitored at all; Jade still had to inject me with blood thinner, which I used to find highly amusing. Dave and Jade were so serious, but sometimes I wailed with uncontrollable giggles as they tried to stab me in the guts - the stroke can make you very childlike at times. I hated having no emotional control.

I had a house to myself and I was beside myself with this. "Whooohoooo! I can watch my own TV and throw the ball for Cody my dog, and watch more TV and emmmm....yes, it quickly became very obvious I needed STRUCTURE!

I decided to write out a timetable like I had in Shents or I would slowly die from endless Judge Judy court cases! No offence meant, of course, Judge! I'd always needed routine in my life. In the building trade or in the British army it's that structure that helps you focus to get the task in hand done! My plan was based on my rehabilitation program on Ward 7.

SPEECH 8-9am – TRYING TO READ OUT LOUD. This would force me to get my lips, tongue, swallowing, breathing, and pronunciation together. I wasn't sure back then, but all I knew was my lungs were burning and it was so hard. I wasn't ever a clever man in life but I knew this much, if it was burning, a muscle was most probably building, so I stuck with it day after day. Screaming too! I had the idea that a baby screams for the first part of its life and all through school playgrounds, and I thought that made perfect sense to me! So... I screamed my wheels off!!! My scream was pathetic, even the dog wasn't sure what to make of it all - was I crying???? Cody didn't know whether to put his head on my lap or run, poor thing.

Well, actually I did end up in tears most times with frustration. How could I be living this life? But when I cried sometimes, it was so loud my soft pallet was engaging; so sometimes I would actually try to get upset, to do it again! This is why sometimes speech therapy is better alone. You need to experiment stupid techniques alongside your pathologist's given exercises! That's what I found, but aphasia after stroke (often called dysphasia) is a result of damage to the language centres of the brain. Understanding, writing, calculation, speaking, reading, gesture, can all be affected - the severity of aphasia varies from person to person depending on the area and brain damage.

Next: LEARNING TO WRITE. Normally ABCs spring to mind. Well, trying to hold and grip a pen was the most seemingly impossible first task! It took the first 20 days or so just to get my thumb to grip against my finger. Some tears there too, I tell ya! I started to hit my right hand most days, repeatedly with my left hand, as the left one had a bit more movement due to all the feeding practice. I was so angry, but I wasn't going to change hands after 33 years! It probably would have been easier, for sure, as I could grip a spoon with my left hand. Pencils, ball point pens were impossible, but with fine liners I could mark the page - just! I remembered the alphabet but hadn't written a letter for a good seven months, the first being 'I' - the simplest, well you would think!!! I obviously found every letter hard and OMG it made me so tired, concentrating on that squeeze and pressure on the page.

We were planning our citizenship later that year, so I was getting in a routine, trying to read out the history of Australia, page by page. I forget a lot now, but I think the arrival of the first fleet of ships from Portsmouth England stuck in my mind, 13th May 1787, to form the penal colony that became the first European settlement in Australia; the first test in my life I got 98% on. I never really did my homework as a kid; I was usually the lad doing lines at break time. This time around, aged 35, I was doing lines because it had become a privilege and not a punishment! Maybe I should have worked harder as a kid, hey; I could have been a Dr Coghlan!

Countless A4 pages full of every letter, week after week, then progressing to actual sentences, usually writing something like "I HATE THIS SHIT! ....I HATE THIS SHIT! ....I HATE THIS SHIT! Or "I WANT MY LIFE BACK... I WANT MY LIFE BACK!" If I had a dollar for every time I blinked those words out!

Cody soon got used to my crazy shouting and screaming like a mad man. He would scratch at the back patio glass door in panic until I let him out. That was the only humour in my day, I think, until Jade arrived home. She had that knack of making me laugh.

I didn't cook back then as I was limited to what was safe, so I lived on Ski yoghurts for a while. I could proudly peel off the paper lid myself, learnt from the ridiculous number of attempts in Shents. Cody's reward for dealing with a screaming lunatic was the 'empty' pot after I'd scraped it.

At times I rested in the sun, just me and Cody; he kept trying to get me to throw the ball like he had remembered in the park and, sure enough, I tried to hold the ball and pathetically launch it. Mostly my fingers wouldn't let go and sometimes this just made me break down into a teary mess again. The simple pleasures were still so far away!

Chapter 23

For a long time, my days involved being trapped in the house, but I was happy just to have some independence back - my own space again. I used to get knocks at the door from different religious groups. In my old life I probably would have said "no thank you" and turned them away politely, but I was pleased to see them, and asked them in for a cuppa every time. We would talk for hours until they got sick of me! They stopped coming after a while when they could see I just wanted to chat! My nasally voice wasn't the easiest to listen to for any more than five minutes I'm sure! The nose clip I was wearing didn't help, the religious guys spent more time looking at that than understanding anything I said!!!! Yet I could always turn to Facebook! Someone would always talk to me on there, I actually found Facebook a great help in my recovery; friends would listen and support me, there are many stroke pages out there too!

I tried not to go on Facebook too much in the day, as it was only going to help me mentally! Well, having said that, that's not strictly true - thinking about it, my typing over the years on my laptop has improved my arms dramatically, but there is the danger of just sitting there all day and not challenging yourself - I see that now.

I wanted to get back to ME, and I was prepared to put the hard yards in to get there, damn it! No one was telling me otherwise, although I broke down countless times a day, sobbing like a baby! I was full of tough moments, then cried so loud followed by uncontrollable hysteria - all within 5 minutes!

My bar was a massive help in my recovery; I built it myself proudly rendering it and tiling the counter. I missed being Pete the Brickie. Wasn't much I couldn't do! I used to wheel my chair up to the bar when Jade was home and, using my hand that *could* lift, grab hold of my bar and drag myself to a standing position. I could stand from all my hard work in Shents. To be safe, I held on with my chair behind me, (brakes on)! I would stare at my bar clock with trembling knees like an electric toothbrush, trying to last a minute or more!

I soon realised that music again would be my focusing weapon, using music like Enigma, Eminem, Metallica, or Epic Score to fuel and harness my focus. I was determined to improve my standing time; my goal was one more minute every day, some days more, depending on sleep or how angry I was! (When you're angry a lot can be accomplished - I learned that alright!)

The euphoric/Celtic/rap/metal charging tunes were really the fuel I needed back then. Almost warp minded, I got very angry, I felt my adrenalin being born again! This was hard to switch off afterwards and with the exhaustion I would sometimes be a bit quick to explode at people. Poor Jade! She often had my emotional atomic outbursts!

The mental battle to control and balance your emotions is something that most people could never understand; it's like someone's flicking switches in your brain, sad, happy, cry, laugh, angry, happy, cry again, laugh some more. You feel angry inside yet sometimes you're laughing - you have absolutely no control, which makes you suddenly express a rage - an uncontrollable, overwhelming rage - you just can't help it and your partner cops it!

When I used to train, I would use memories I'd seen in Shents. This I used as serious fuel, as it hurt me a lot; those memories made me angry. "WHY? WHY? WHY??? I asked above.

I saw a lady once, as I lay motionless in physio on a plinth; she was crying with her husband as the physio was trying to work with her, learning to move again. She had literally half her head missing and hardly any hair. She was trying to learn to use the remaining half of her brain. I also saw a young girl whose face had been scraped off, no skin. It was the most shocking thing I think I've ever seen, she was crying with a nurse trying to console her - GOD BLESS NURSES EVERYWHERE. THANKYOU!

I'm trying to control my tears as I write this; these memories will stay with me forever. I didn't realise until many years later after waking up crying that I was suffering with post-traumatic stress disorder. I took Zopiclone sleeping pills for almost 3 years! Anyone who's lived in my world will know it eventually makes you hard; I had to be someone else to get through this. I'm not talking about the film star Jason Statham hard, either! I mean upstairs (in the old think tank). It changes you inside. You look at the world differently, like that film Matrix; not that we see things in digits, but you see the good in the world more, as you're far more grateful for everything you have, even if that's nothing! You learn to value the simple things and you start to realise there are so many wonderful people out there suffering with something too. I find I take the time now to talk to absolutely everyone, whereas before I'd just want to get home for that Scotch 'n Coke 'n a smoke at my bar.

Jade gets frustrated with me a lot. I'm always talking to strangers everywhere; getting anywhere with me can take all day sometimes! But the way I see it now is, I CAN TALK! It's a gift, and I didn't really see it before! It's a real privilege we take so lightly, as we don't always remember all those years of learning and struggling to master that skill and 'privilege'. I learned everything twice! I should be really clever now, ey? "Can't work that part out!"

Jade and I had some scuffles as time moved on. I was becoming obsessed with my goals and she was very tired of trying to keep a roof over our head. This frustrated me more because I couldn't make everything ok! Any man would get upset about this! This pushed me harder yet I think started to push us further apart. She was so good to me and I didn't see it back then through my mental struggle and pain. She was the one who forced me to talk without my nose peg; I didn't have the confidence in public, because of a fear of not being understood. Very frightening times! I had no confidence outside the Shents bubble really. Everyone knew me there in rehab; I was a freak out in Perth (I felt).

It was about that time I had a phone call from Danny, my old UK wing man from our teens. Danny and Andrea, 'his lady', wanted to visit. It was the most exciting news for us. We had been through such a tough seven months. Then a few weeks later, Jenny and Matt came too! They cheered me up, always did, and it was a positive focus for us at the time. Friends often don't realise just what impact they can have on a relationship after stroke or trauma - so please play a part in your fallen friends' lives. It's not always easy, but even a phone call or regular emails or texts. So many people, who were not in my last seven years, will not be in my future; as I found out just who wanted to be in my life! It's very sad indeed.

On knowing my friends were coming, I was fuelled again. I tried to help Jade more in the house, attempting to wash up all the time as my job; what a contribution I was making, Whoopee-do!! But it was hard as hell to stand there while using your arms and hands!

Muti-tasking was a mega hard skill to take on after only just being home from quadriplegia a few months. Every task was impossible. I came a cropper one day and it's a bit embarrassing, but after my story so far it hardly matters!

I was keeping a diary and writing the first part of this book in 2012. I was concentrating so hard I didn't feel that feeling you feel when you need to 'go' – yes, I don't mean a pee either. Before I realised it was too late! Because I'd been sitting down for so long I should have noticed, but often when you're in a wheelchair your bowel movements are not so obvious. Shit! What should I do now? I promised I wouldn't get out of my chair while Jade's at work! (I had transferred a few times but not full of mess!) There was No Way I was just sitting there in case somebody came and saw me with that smell in my pants. Only one thing I could do! Break my promise and get myself undressed. I'd only let Jade see me once in that state during my recovery - that was back in Charlies and, as you know, I always kept my shorts on, so I knew I could deal with this if I was careful. Amazing what you can do when you're in the shit, ey! Haha.

Trainers I could kick off thanks to the great Alisha; I used my bar to pull my pants down then wheeled my way over to the washer. Yes! I did it! Very proud of myself - now for the powder! It was in the left-hand cupboard at the bottom and, in my eagerness, as I leaned over to get it I bloody fell in the cupboard didn't I - washing powder absolutely everywhere! I was having a crappy day alright!

Dog in my face, trying desperately to get back in my wheelchair, full of powder, stark naked.... Thank God this is a book, not a movie!

Right! Washer on, get back in my chair and hoover quickly - Jade's just a few hours away. I can do this, she'll never know! Back room, where the Hoover was kept; I could just about lift it - Yes! Then BANG!!! Damn, I had now taken the paintwork off the door-frame! Aaaarrrhhh, bloody great!! This is bollocks!!!! "F***in' hell!" (If you were my dog, that was the most frequent scream of frustration!)

Still naked in my chair, half full of powder, dragging the Hoover behind me, I started to vacuum up the mess I had made. Eureka! On managing to put fresh shorts on I'd pulled it off, with only a damaged door-frame as evidence! So, not to lose face, when Jade came home and asked "How was your day?" I replied, "Yes, yes, busy typing, you know me! "Any problems?" "No, no, 'course not," I fibbed, keeping my pride intact.

Although I tried to make humour out of everything, I was hurting inside. I felt like a monster. In my heart I honestly believed that I had no purpose anymore, that no one understood how I felt, constantly fighting depression, fatigue and vulnerability! The need to find hope and strength in a new day was all I had to live for. This time of my life was about ME ME ME! I feel guilty now, but it had to be that way, you understand? Survival in the mental sense!

Exercise until my muscles burned was the closest thing to remembering old days when I was strong. My legs used to burn the same way on platoon marches in full combats, or when holding that stance in karate! I knew the feeling so well and remembering that feeling became my only way out!

I wanted ME back. I thought I could fix everything by achieving that very goal. "I MUST GET ME BACK!" was the only phrase in my head; not listening to reason... stubborn as a mule they say! And my obsession grew stronger by the day! I wasn't, and WE most certainly were not, getting stronger either!

I was desperate for this to be over. It's so unfair because I had to put the time in, but I had nothing left to give anyone afterwards and for years that was the case. I guess I was like Fharlap, that awesome race horse in the 1930s "blinkers on an' full charge ahead." I couldn't consider what it must have been like for Jade.

Standing time at the bar was gradually increased week by week to an amazing whole 15 mins! This made me so hungry for MORE! Could I make 30 minutes? Could I make an hour? I don't need to run through the monthly minute chart staring at that damn clock. Needless to say, the end was too far away to visualise; desperately I clung to the belief that somewhere in the distance my life would be waiting.

When you have goals you're very warp-minded. That's healthy in a way I think, but.... I was so tired every day by the time Jade got home, after being on her feet for 8 hours, she was getting a bit sick and tired of holding us together – mainly just tired. She knew I was trying, and my saying "I just gotta beat my time, just gotta, just gotta!" was not exactly what she needed after her arduous shift.

I didn't have anything else to talk about; for me it was repetitive bad ass tunes to push through the shaking legs every day - and the burn, that was it! I'd lost the power of normal conversation. I'd lost my personality for a long time back then. Anyway - positive thoughts!

Danny coming over was the only event I had to look forward to and I wanted to walk on my own, to show off and to do stuff when he arrived. I'd never done this without Alisha behind me or Jade holding my hand!

I began upping the anti, pushing the limits to the next stage! So one sunny weekend I cut the grass in my electric chair - getting stuck a few times, admittedly, but loving the smell of freshly cut grass, minus the odd gift Cody had left for me - like they do! My wheels had gone through some that day! Jade was not impressed when I drove through the kitchen not realising! Oops!!!

Crap just seemed to follow me that year, ey! After Dave, my house mate, had kindly cleaned my wheels, I pulled up in the middle of the garden, opened my foot plates, checked the brakes were on and the power was off. I was ready to take my first step alone! No physio, no counter, no hand. Just me and balance! I just had to know if I could do a few steps, turn around and sit back down again. Very ballsy! My heart was beating like I was on a rollercoaster ride. I don't suppose many people reading this can quite understand just how scared you feel when your arms can't break your fall.

Yes!!!!! This was my Rocky scene: "Yo Adrian! I DID IT!!!" One small step for Pete, one giant leap from LIS in late 2011! With my proud day of two massive steps forward, two steps back, I was euphoric!

Guess what I did for the next month!!!! By early 2012 I had gone from the length of the garden to the park – a 1000 metres round trip! I also found the confidence to talk to other dog walkers – thanks to my own mutt Cody who, after his $10,000 leg operation, was by my side, limping along with me! Divine justice in a way! I sincerely believe by making the choice not to have him put down, I survived!!! I still remember his nose in my face during my coma! That stuff spooks me out; in fact, I've become very spiritual these days.

I started following my gut feelings; the aboriginal elders believe we have 3 ways of thinking!

*our head

*our heart

*our gut

Two of these will lead to your future - your heart and your gut! They say white fellas (as they call us) think too much with our heads! Our heads question too much, sometimes stopping us, just in case THIS happens or THAT happens!

Anxiety, depression, all negative emotions stop you. Our think tank can make us too focused on money and you start missing life itself. And not just money – I'm even talking about that girl you failed to contact because you didn't want to come across as a stalker! Just follow your feelings every time! Let feelings guide you to where you're meant to be! I sound like Gandalf these days, the wise wizard. Through loss you sure learn.

We were maxed out on a credit card but seeing Cody walking again (limping), beside a guy that wasn't ever meant to walk either (also limping), we were quite the talk of my neighbourhood. Me and Codes!

I met some nice people in that park; they all seemed to have the right advice for stroke, thinking they were helping, of course, but really having no idea! One guy actually told me that walking through morning dew in bare feet will heal you! What the....? Yeah, ok then, I'll try magic mushrooms too, mate! There are crazy people out there, that's for sure!

I haven't mentioned outpatients' rehabilitation yet. To be honest, I wasn't sure if what I had to say was constructive. I didn't want to complain, as we are very lucky to have such a health system. But in the defence of strokies out there, there's not enough time given.... It wasn't working for me.

Let me explain. Twice a week a Maxi taxi (a bus with a lift at the back) used to pick me up, then pick up someone else, then someone else - about 6 people in all I think! The journey took about 1 hour 30 mins, followed by 1 hour in the physio gym with the physios, who were awesome, but I feel, overstretched. So you would end up waiting around for quite a while. My conclusion, three hours travelling time, one hour gym time, with less than 15 mins of physio – 1 on 1 time!

Like I said, I'm not a clever man but I worked out I could use this 4 hours more wisely at home, so I decided to set up my own exercise area next to my bar! Dave set up a rail on the wall for me to grip: a 50mm foam exercise mat, a pulley system created from pulleys and carabiners and rope, all from the hardware shop. Completing my home-made equipment were physio bands, a wooden pole, a few light weights and Velcro to counterbalance my arm on the pulley. I lived in this small area for at least 1 hour a day, then took my slow, leg-dragging walk to the park with Cody. The remaining time was spent writing and improving my speech, giving me total control of my own therapy! I've always worked hardest on my own; I focus better. Even when reading information I need to be alone to absorb everything with no distractions. My short attention span goes back to school days, passing notes to girls instead of listening. Ha-ha.

But seriously, if we want to improve our system, we must be prepared to help ourselves – at least that's my opinion. Fortunately for me, I was no stranger to exercise and knew enough to avoid taking risks. I'm not saying everyone should do this - it could go wrong, of course - but you know your own body. All I'm saying is, don't just rely on the struggling health system and weekly physio sessions - put the time in yourself, AS WELL!

Chapter 24

Except for the year (2012), I honestly can't remember the finer details of Daniel's arrival. I only know it was a pivotal point in my home rehabilitation crusade. First of all, he got me signed up to my local gym, which, as mentioned earlier and unbeknown to Danny, was to become my salvation, my church! My future sanity! He also made me a 'thank you' video for my physio Alisha; that meant so much to me back then - "THANKS, BRO!"

During his visit, he took me down the Swanee on my 18ft half-cab boat which, to my frustration, had been slowly dying on my drive ever since my stroke. Once he got my engine going again, we cruised along the Swan River here in Perth, right in front of the city. Then we went golfing, with me driving the buggy! YAY! Awesome! First time behind the wheel again, whizzing across the green - I felt so alive!

I didn't feel a freak with Danny – yet I was not yet comfortable with me! It takes a long time to come to terms with the massive physical and mental changes caused by stroke. We laughed so much those few short weeks, but then Danny and I always had that click. You only get a handful of friends in life like that, mainly because you spend so much time with your mates in your teens – before life gets all serious – time you rarely get again, although I'm lucky to have so many great friends.

Not that I go out drinking as much now. A lot of friends come with drink, I've found - all laughter when you're on top, yet strangely absent when your wheels fall off, as my sister Vicky says so wisely!

I actually got a par 3 that day on Marangaroo Golf Course, it was unbelievable! Yeah! Yeah! Honestly! I couldn't believe it myself, being unable to hit the driver in the right direction! And the fish was this big…. I know what ya thinking!

First swing – the ball bounced off the tree on the left of the fairway, right into the middle. Second swing -

onto the green, just! Then, with one smooth tap, I drove it into the hole like a pro! Watch out Tiger Woods! Oh yeah that's right! Danny had this new super awesome looking driver; he couldn't wait to show me how far he could smash the ball.

So he's there doing the knee bent thing, looking down the fairway, looking down at the ball, then up, you know - all professional like. The he absolutely launches this ball at Mach 1, only to smack a kangaroo in the neck as it lay basking in the sun! Hahaha! And you know what? That roo never moved a muscle! They're bloody tough animals for sure! We were laughing so hard – but only when we knew the little hopper was unfazed!

The weeks flew, and all too soon Daniel and Andrea are catching their flight to Dubai, leaving me in great spirits. I'll never forget that Danny!

Before our friends all left we hired a spar, to give them a decent West Aussie send off. Julia and Sean were also very much in our lives and had layed on a fancy dress party, with a HEAVEN AND HELL theme. Danny as Chucky the killer doll, me as Pinhead from Hell Raiser, and the girls as angels (of course!) It took several hours for Jade to put the pins in my latex skin and get me ready - I looked amazing! Pinhead in the wheelchair, Chucky walking next to me with a big plastic knife and Dave as Freddy Krueger! Great night! As for Julia, 70 years old and still partying hard; unbelievable woman!

I drank scotch that night, something I said I'd never do again, but that night I almost forgot life was so crap - God bless my mates for that!

Chapter 25

Weeks after my wingman left I was back into my rehab, motivation tank well and truly refilled. My first mission was to see if I could walk to the local gym that I was now a proud member of! If so, I'd be able to spend my days in the pool instead of my little rehab area! People to share my days with again, new faces even!

I had to be really careful, though, because the road was only 2 metres from the pavement and I didn't trust that foot of mine - the slightest thing could bring me down. I actually fell twice in the first month, dropping like a scout walker from Star Wars, imaginary cables fired around my legs, with a Chewbacca sound effect on the way down. But my park walks had paved the way over the months, so I didn't often fall. Glad I put the time in on the grass first!

Another obstacle to overcome was my fear of water. Although I took a massive risk just getting there, for the first few months I clung to the side of the pool at the shallow end, spending most of the time in the sauna and Jacuzzi where I could relax, just sitting and thinking for hours about what I'd been through since my stroke! Sometimes the pool area was so quiet there'd only be three or four of us. Most people had jobs to go to and lives to live, so it was the perfect time for me – usually 10am-2pm. Yes, that's a ridiculous amount of time, but going home was often very daunting; cocooned by my surroundings, I was a new person... Lost in water! Astrologers say Cancer crabs take to water in times of stress; well that certainly applies to me - a water sign through and through. I usually find a level with everyone there, having lived in water for at least a year before making it upstairs to the gym.

I became known to all the gym staff, "Hi Pete! How are you?" Words that meant so much to me after months of trauma! My struggle days had at last made me a part of something again!

On growing slightly more confident, I used flotation noodles to help lift my legs, placing the noodle under my knees while trying not to lose hold of the pool's tiled edge. Although fear of drowning restricted me to safe exercises such as heel raises, the water really reduced my stress, releasing he pressure inside of me (I was like an atomic bomb!) It was something Jade needed too, actually, had she only been given a chance!

People don't think about the partner as much, as "they're living a normal life compared to you, so they'll be ok!" WELL THEY'RE NOT!!! Loved ones become carers and carers need help sometimes – more help than they get now. Yes, there's a carer's allowance you can apply for in most developed countries, But that's not the be all and end all! There should be rest breaks and a lot more community support out there.

Incidentally Jade never qualified for the carer's payment for two reasons: by doing as much over-time as she could, to pay for my gym and rehab needs, she earned $200 too much per week; not realising that if you worked fewer hours you qualify! The same old story, kill yourself trying and it seems the system is against you.

The other reason I believe we didn't qualify was down to one simple question: "Can the person in care cut a pork chop?" Well naturally I was proud to say "Yes" - making a real mess, of course, and only if it wasn't too fatty - but in truth I could hardly use my right arm and hand at all. Pride was my enemy.

No doubt I answered a few more questions like this; proof you need help when filling in forms. At such times, there should be an advocate for every single person struggling with such bureaucracy. Ridiculously frustrating!

Every second day, I went to the Goodlife Pool to get my fix. Limping through the passageways and back streets of Marangaroo and getting to know every tree, every hole and every feature of the route. Confronting another person, particularly if they were young, caused some anxiety, fear of being so vulnerable. One woman stopped to ask me the time but, when I tried to answer as best I could in my nasally Darth Vader voice, she froze in horror and with a curt "I don't speak English!" walked off quickly! She bloody asked me in English in the first place! That really vexed me and put a downer on my whole day. If I hadn't already been conscious enough of my speech impediment, her reaction would have made me feel like a monster!

I had also stopped using my nose peg at the time, but carried it just in case, as my confidence was constantly under attack by such reactions. But you have to keep trying, because by staying silent, there's a danger of going backwards. Use it or lose it, they say, ey! Take it from me, talk to everyone who will listen until they get sick of you. Practice, practice, practice!

My first year of recovery was so mundane yet, towards the end of 2012, I was setting myself weekly challenges, one being to walk as far as my Mum's house in Alexander Heights. This was bordering on crazy as I was doing 2.5km there, then after lunch another 2.4km back! Everyone was worried. I'd text Mum from a bench every few bus stops to say where I was. "Almost half way, Mum." "At the traffic lights in 5, Mum."

I don't think any of my loved ones were happy with the idea, but I wouldn't be told - glad about that today! I was determined to prove to myself I could go further and further! I didn't have a chip on my shoulder or anything; I just so badly wanted to escape this nightmare. There was only one option - one more step was one step closer to my new distant self. Plugged into my hard-core tunes, which inspired me, I kept going, step by step!

All sounds heroic, I guess, for LIS sufferers. That was also my motivation at the time - to see how far I could go and prove to the medical world that, given time and obsessive behaviour, "Hey the brain can come back!" I was determined to prove we could recover!

But my attitude came at a price – a painful one at times. Overconfidence caught me out, and the odd missed-step caused me to "come the occasional cropper!" One time, my foot caught on the path, allowing no time even to scream as I crumbled helplessly onto my knee, falling forward at such speed the stones and grit embedded in my grazed wrist and patella, which I thought I'd broken, the pain was so bad. I realise now, that could have set me back a long time. In panic, I tried to get up quickly so nobody could see what had happened! Only to fall again! I then began crawling to the nearest lamp post for assistance; all the while with cars passing, their drivers most probably thinking I was drunk! Nobody stops these days, especially for someone with a shaved head!

Yes, the year was long, and after walking week after week, month after month, my life began to feel like that of a hamster on a wheel. Of course I was grateful, thanking God every day for being alive, so much so I cried frequently, but I was running out of fuel again, feeling mentally flat. I couldn't imagine Jade's frustration, me spending my time in the pool or walking daily, then too tired to even talk or help with dinner. Although I did try; doing the shopping once a week in between my marathon walks, filling my backpack with spuds and veg - God, that was heavy! I tried for hours to hold the potatoes and peel them - when you can hardly use your hands, that's a very loving mission indeed - but such small contributions didn't impress for long.

Maybe the power above was dangling carrots every now and then, as every time I lost my drive - I mean totally lost all hope - things happened. For example, I had this idea to walk for a disabled friend I'd shared a room with, Ryan Marron (who I mentioned earlier) a policeman who contracted encephalitis (inflammation of the brain) from a mosquito bite. I wanted to try to make a 7km walk for Ryan. I knew I could walk 5km with breaks, although 7km was pushing my limits back then. Even so, with friends and loved ones behind me I was up for it; horns raised like a bull, not as confident but full charge as always. Act first, think later, that's me! Well, I do have these ideas!

As usual, Jade was willing to walk with me, helping me achieve my goal for Ryan and hopefully raise a few thousand dollars in the process. It was a long walk, 7km in all, starting from Hillary's boat harbour and continuing along the coast to Scarborough. But if I felt nervous about this challenge, I couldn't complain about the weather. It was a beauty of a day, and all our friends had come to give us a good send-off - including Sally Allen representing Northern Suburbs Stroke Group. Little did I know Sally had tipped off the media about this monster goal of mine and, although I didn't realise it at the time, I was apparently the first man to walk 7km just 6 months after leaving hospital with LIS. NO CLOT BUSTING DRUGS EITHER - and mostly with my own rehab!

After being so helpless, raising money for a fellow roommate along with the sheer physical challenge really felt awesome, although halfway through I thought I wouldn't make it, as heavy rain started to pelt down on me. The deluge lasted about 25-30 minutes and the T-shirt I had on was so heavy and sticking to me. Thank God it eventually subsided! My body heat then dried me out over the following few kilometres - I had to dig deep that day!

Big smiling face, blistered feet forgotten, I made it! I had smashed my goal! And, if proof were needed, there's a video of me limping across the Finish line in Scarborough; although looking at it online now, I could've done with a few tips from Jenny Craig's weight loss program. WHAT A POT BELLY! I was E.T. alright!

Thanks to all my friends that day who shared my walk for Ryan. I proudly posted my video to show all my nurses in Shents it was worth answering my call bell 1000 times and giving me all that personal care I needed - not to mention feeding me 3 times a day! "THANK YOU" x

The magnitude of that day fuelled me for weeks after, but life was far from sweet! Sometime later, Jade and I had an uncomfortable talk. She was upset, and rightly so, because she was working so hard but there was never anything left. I was hurting inside to see her so sad and I felt really helpless. Other than train harder and longer, what else could I do?

I often talked via Facebook to my father in Thailand about my situation, pouring out my heart for hours. "Dad, I hate my life! I can't help Jade - she's struggling so hard to look after me. What can I do?"

After a while, he came up with a solution which stunned me! "Son! Do you think you and Jade might be able to run a little café?" Not only did Jade have plenty of experience, be she was sharp with money - always the brains, for sure. 'Yes Dad," I answered, intrigued by his suggestion. "Well Son, I'm willing to help you both - if you'll consider moving to Thailand!" Oh.....my......God! "Really, Dad?!" "Yes, really! Speak to Jade and let me know what her thoughts are. Then get back to me if you think it will help you." "I will, Dad, I will. Wow, thanks Dad!" I was truly gob-smacked. "Ok, Son. I'll try to help you. You know I love you both."

Shutting my laptop, I truly believed, I had the answer to our prayers and couldn't wait to tell Jade. Visions of happiness and a wonderful future welded into my mind before she'd even arrived home. In fact, I had it all planned out years into the future. This was how it was going to be – the glorious Thailand life style, my way out of a drowning ship. What could possibly go wrong?

Chapter 26

Jade didn't quite react as I expected. I was desperate for her to like the idea, but she was a very calculated thinker. Before the stroke, we'd enjoyed fantastic times in Thailand - met friends, had wild drinking bouts, ridden miles on the back of Dad's motor bike through fields of coconuts and pineapples.... Ahhhhh the warm air and smell of coconut husks burning on fires! An absolute dream even now! Somehow, I forgot I was just out of a wheelchair and had serious speech issues! I suppose I should have been scared. And there were other problems which Jade was quick to highlight.

"What about Cody? What about our home, your Mum, your sister, our friends?" I hadn't thought that deeply at the time! The possibility of running away from this life was all I'd considered, and Thailand seemed to be the answer. I begged Jade!

"It'll be ok. Dave will look after the house and Cody! A few years that's all! It'll be good for us! We can get married while were there! This could be the most amazing thing, Jade! Come on - trust me!"

Any of my close friends can tell you that I can be quite the salesman and irritatingly persistent until I seal the deal! Ha-ha. Besides, I honestly believed we were going to play out the idylls of happiness frolicking through my head! With such conviction and powers of persuasion over the next week or so, I managed to get Jade to say 'Yes', although I suspect this was less due to my sales pitch than Jade's willingness to make me happy. I was not myself, back then, and I was desperate to make us strong again.

I lay awake with thoughts of what steps needed to be taken! "Ok I can sell my boat! I can have a garage sale and empty my shed - must be a few quid there! Maybe Dave will buy our stuff!"

In one night I had it all worked out; I was prepared to give up our home in Marrangaroo where we'd been so happy for seven years. Seven years of memories, things we'd worked hard for. I just didn't see it. I'd have done anything to leave my cursed life after the stroke.

I still trained hard in Goodlife's pool, planning and scheming, plotting my escape while moving my arms as best I could in the water! "I'll empty my shed in the morning and then price everything up. Yeah, that's what I'll do! The camping stuff is almost new – should get a good price for that. Oh yeah, my cement mixer is only 6 months old - that'll fetch $300 surely, it cost me $900!"

I was a man possessed!! Anyone reading this, who's had an illness, will understand my frame of mind; I just needed to get away from this nightmare I'd been living for the past year. Things didn't matter. In my head, my family, friends and dog will all be there after I get better in Thailand! I WILL be fixed! Thailand will make things okay! I know it!

Dave was brilliant. Not only was he prepared to buy our fridge, washing machine, TV, sofa, and the entire contents of our home, he was also interested in buying our rental! I arranged to sell our 4x4 to my mate Duncan, as I owed him $10,000. My boat was up for sale. Looking back, I was an absolutely desperate man who was, quite frankly, far from sound-minded. Jade should have put her foot down and made a stand to this craziness. She'd moved across the Earth with me and trusted me so far - but this! This was utter lunacy!

My mum and sister tried to talk to me, to no avail. I wouldn't like to have known myself back then; I'm ashamed to have been so self-absorbed, but I wanted to fix us. I needed to fix ME, do whatever was necessary, at all costs!

Dave gave us the $3000 up front, enough to buy tickets to our new life, while Dad organised the work visas through his company. Jade gave her notice in at work, my 18ft half cab boat was sold for $500 and the 4x4 was being exchanged in the last week so we could still use it. Plants, bric a brac, building materials left over from jobs, cement bags, tie wires, endless tubes of silicone, every tool I had - anything to make a dollar. I was selling our life for a dream! But there was no turning back now!

In the middle of this came another disaster. Limping about in the dark at 5am, I labelled my shed tools and laid everything out for the first punters to arrive that morning. Stupidly, I tried to carry a plank to place on trestles and, forgetting my disabilities, stumbled badly, landing head-first into the sandy sun-dried grass! I didn't tell people how many times I came a cropper; I guess I've always been too proud to admit my failures.

That time was very, very emotional. Everything happened so quickly, it's hard to recall the sequence of events, although I'm really surprised how much I have retained considering I'm still googling the spelling of some of these words - at 40 years of age! It's quite astounding how much information we collect without thinking about it really. I've managed to retain all my memories, happily for me, as some strokes can take them away! During my hospital stay, one man got regular visits from his family but had no idea who they were! I used to wonder whether he was he luckier than I was because he could feed himself – a hard call to make if you were in my shoes! Memories or the use of your arm?

Having been granted our permanent resident residency one week before my locked in brain-stem stroke, Jade and I were allowed to have a work visa overseas. I fully intended to call Australia home afterwards. Perth itself I wasn't too sure about at first, although a beautiful place, the sun was so intense in the summer you could actually cook an egg on the car bonnet - no word of a lie! I tried it!

We didn't find it easy to leave friends back in the mother land either. That's why the English are often referred to as yoyos; back and forward then back again! The blue skies and beautiful beaches versus family and friends they leave behind - not as black and white as that either! Fresh social circles can be difficult, and genuine friendships take many years to forge. Only through life's ups and downs will you find your best buddies and no matter how pretty or exciting a place might be, trying to adjust can sometimes be too hard for many! And, as if life wasn't tricky enough, amongst all the plans I only had to complicate things further!

"Why don't we get married?" Dad and his wife Noi were all for this idea, even offering to pay for the event as their wedding gift to us. After all, we were already engaged so why not make an honest woman of Jade, the woman who'd helped me claw my way back from hell. Recovering from locked in syndrome! Selling our lives! Moving to Thailand! It seemed the logical thing to do! There wasn't much going on, so why not, ey? Ha-ha.

I knew I wanted to marry Jade when I first met her 20 years ago. Looking back, there was never a question about that; over the previous 15 years, absolutely nothing was more important to me than Jade. But now I wanted ME back in my life just as much as I wanted Jade! In the wake of the stroke, every single decision was now geared towards recovery and my obsession with reaching new goals.

As for the wedding, I didn't just see this as a special union before God, although I had wanted this to happen since I first clocked eyes upon her in 1996. Marrying Jade had somehow become another personal goal! To walk down the aisle witnessed by loved ones who'd been told I would probably never walk again, was to me the proud moment for which I'd been fighting for a year; in many ways the equivalent of winning a heavyweight title belt, screaming "Yo, Jadey! I DID IT!" Too many Rocky films, I know!

From blinking out "I WILL get back to you!" on one of my brave mornings in G51, to actually standing on my own two feet and saying "I DO!"

Looking back at my communication book (in March 2018) seven years afterwards, is still an extremely painful thing to do, as I can feel my emotion at that time and probably always will.

We couldn't legally marry in Thailand if we wanted it to be internationally recognised, so we legalised our union at the Registry Office in Perth with only a handful of people attending.... no favouritism here. Those invited couldn't attend the Thailand ceremony that Dad and Noi were in the early stages of planning. So, a few weeks before take-off, there we were, on the top floors of Perth Registry Office overlooking the beautiful Swan River, getting a bird's eye view of the speed boats and buying our $500 wedding ticket. To me it felt like taking a ticket at the deli counter, then waiting for our slot! Pretty romantic, hey? Actually, once in the beautiful room it really was! The aerial view of Perth's River is, from any angle, totally breath taking!

Proudly, I repeated the words of the celebrant and signed the book after what was, looking back, a beautiful ceremony, simple as it was.

Life has a way of teaching us, as we stumble through!

Chapter 27

BING BONG! "Flight to Bangkok Suvarnabhumi International Airport, will all passengers please proceed to gate number 15 - now boarding." No turning back now! It wasn't until we were 38,000ft up that I started feeling anxious, but kept telling myself "We'll be alright. Nice coffee shop in Thailand - sweet!"

After finishing a glass of wine (you know those tiny bottles you get) I'd just asked for another when the stewardess came back and said, very politely, "Excuse me, Sir, would you mind coming to the rear of the aircraft, please"? "Yes of course," I said with an inquisitive, nasally voice! Everyone looked at me as I followed her down the aisle with my very distinctive limp towards the curtained area at the back or the plane where food and drinks are dispensed. To my horror, there were 5 stewards and beefy security guys waiting for me, looking like extras from Border Control on TV. "Someone's planted drugs on me!" I thought, "Please God No!" I knew I should have bought expensive locks for my luggage!

At the time, the Schapelle Corby story was all over the news – on her way to Indonesia, a bulk-load of marijuana was found in her surfboard. She was subsequently tried, convicted and imprisoned in Bali.

"Sir, we feel you have had too much to drink!" Too much? I'd only had one glass!

"But Sir, you've ordered 3 so far."

"Yes, two for my wife and one for me!"

"But Sir, the stewards say you're slurring your words!"

I smiled, relieved to know it wasn't a drug rap and then replied, somewhat embarrassed: "I had a major stroke which left me with speech problem!" The tense eyes became relaxed smiles; they were probably feeling a little embarrassed too, I think, because they gave us special service during the rest of our transfer flight to Kuala Lumpur.

I have been stupid many times through my stroke. Not taking advice, or help; I was always right. Like I said, pride was my downfall, as I found out that day.

My behaviour on landing at Kuala Lumpur International Airport was probably the mother of all stubborn, stupid mistakes I had made so far! As the door opened, I expected to see a cube tunnel but steps were being attached instead. Not only that, to my horror it was raining hard, a full on tropical downpour and I began to panic! This was not good, as when I panicked my right leg stiffened! Neurological problems can make your body do things you don't want when you're scared or your adrenaline starts to flow! My option of wheelchair assistance was gone, and I still didn't say I needed help! What a stupid, stupid man I've been! I'd refused this option because I wasn't in a chair anymore. After months of fighting so hard to walk, my electric toothbrush leg-shaking days had gone and, although the chair would have been a massive help, I felt it was a backwards move. Yet I'd have given anything to be pushed in a wheelchair at this moment....OMG! JESUS put your wings around me! Seeing the panic on my face, Jade tried not to get mad at me for getting into 'another fine mess' due my stupid, bloody pride! It was like a Laurel and Hardy movie – but without the laughter. No laughter, even now!

I was so lucky that day. Jade took all the bags and I gripped the handrail for my very life, going backwards for safety, holding all the other passengers up and feeling very stupid and very pathetic. The queue behind me must have numbered 200 (at a guess), as there were steps both sides and I believe a 747 can accommodate 416 passengers in a typical three-class layout.

There was more pressure that day than in all of my life I think, I just couldn't fall down 20 odd steel checker-plated steps today, "Please God, please!" I begged, fearing I'd run out of prayer cards by now! I saw Jade with her small, slender frame struggling with our heavy bags, an image that will forever be burned into my mind with sorrow and for which I hate myself to this day! "I am so sorry Jade!"

I'll spare you from the drama of each terrifying step down to the tarmac. I obviously made it, as I'm drinking my coffee, writing this with shame. Had I slipped I would be dead, I think and Jade would be a widow! 20 0dd treads of steel-checker plate steps would have been most unforgiving I'm sure, for a man with a leg like a plank!

"We need this Jade!" still echoes in my mind. I really did think back then my life had been cursed! Mainly because of my stupid pride to win! In fact, being competitive almost killed me. At 17, I was your typical boy racer with more nerve than nous – and a Ford Orion injection Ghia! Not a good combination, especially when dragging with an ASTRA GTE at 70mph on a damp country night. I lost badly – ending up in an unforgiving stone wall!

The wind screen exploded, glass shattered everywhere, cutting my girlfriend Nicky's face! No scars, thank God, and we're still great friends today; SORRY Nicky! X. Whatever possessed me to be such an arse?! Unfortunately, it's only when we grow older we see how fragile life is, becoming very embarrassed by our younger selves. I was chewing glass myself that night – talk about the skin of my teeth! The impact should have killed me, but it wasn't the only time I've cheated death!

Talking of glass, by the way, I've gotta tell you about another brush with the Grim Reaper – really seems out to get me, that guy! Before my stroke, Jade and I wanted to check out Bali like everyone in Western Australia seems to do – it's very cheap from Perth! We'd booked this new hotel in Legian, which looked awesome, as they always do online and, to be fair, it looked pretty good on arrival too. However, it had only opened the previous month, so a few projects were unfinished, which was probably why it was such a cheap deal.

We were early they said, "The room isn't quite ready. Please take a seat, Sir." As a Bali style tea was served, we looked around the beautiful reception, feeling proud of our choice. "Oh yes, Jade! This'll do!" I picked up a magazine to see what this hotel had in store for us. "Listen to this, Jade!" I began to read the blurb on Page 1 which boasted rooms with balconies "overlooking the well-kept beaches, gardens with pools, 3 restaurants, entertainment..." But Jade had her mind on other things. "Just popping to the loo," she said, leaving me to continue my literary pursuit.

I'd got halfway through Page 2 when... BANG!!!! "WHAT THE...!" There was a massive, MASSIVE explosion. I didn't have time to be scared, or even to think. All I remember was scrambling over the yellow sofa against the wall in reception - or was it a back flip? Yes, that sounds better!

The amount of glass that fell from the air that day was, at a guess, close to 6-7 tons! YES, THE ROOF COLLAPSED ON ME - toughened glass at that - causing millions of shards to hail down across the lobby with a terrible sound. My years as a glass-fitter with Perth CBD told me the glass hadn't been packed right, and giant tubular-shaped bells hanging from the middle and swaying in the wind had caused the domed roof to blow!

Jade returned, gazed at me in shock and her eyes said it all, "I LEAVE YOU ALONE FOR TWO BLOODY MINUTES!!"

The hotel staff were quick to ask if everyone was okay, which thankfully we were. What really upset me was they offered us water - bloody WATER!!!! The roof falls on you and they offer you water!!!!! There was only one reply to that. "Could I have a Johnny Walker and coke, please?" Well, who wouldn't? – does wonders for shock!

Incidentally the hotel was like Fawlty Towers that week, Apart from the roof caving in, I got poisoned by prawns and found a nail sticking out from the bridge in the pool. Imagine if I hadn't spotted it; must have been from the form work, I guessed, I'd done a bit of concreting. New hotels, I think I'll pass on them in future!

And, as I refuse to believe my Jean-Claude van Damme days have gone, I avoid glass hotels to this day!

BING BONG. "This is your captain speaking. Please fasten your seat belts, ladies and gentleman. We will be approaching Suvarnabhumi International airport in 30 minutes time. It's currently 36^{0}C and sunny in Bangkok, 62% humidity, wind 11km/h! "We thank you for travelling Thai airways today and hope you'll fly with us again soon. Hope you have a pleasant stay." BING BONG...

The connecting flight from Kuala Lumpur was finally over, much to my relief, as I wasn't feeling great at all. Fatigue had me in a bag over its shoulder, my body was shutting down, but the airport smell kept me going. It's a smell I've always loved, taking me back to my baggage handling days at Manchester airport months before joining the army. It was an exciting job for a young lad; you got to push back the aircrafts to runways - well I didn't do that personally, but assisted the tug driver by pulling out the pin once the aircraft was in position. Felt such a rush from giving the pilot a thumps up, indicating he was clear for take-off, and feeling and smelling the air from the engines.

And then there was 'chocking. Believe me, chocking a Cathay Pacific was like nothing else. Chocks are giant rubber wedges placed in front and behind the massive wheels. It's really exciting standing in front of a Boeing 767 as it taxis along in front of you! Whooooo! Yeah! Then it's your job to chock the wheels and give the pilots the thumbs down – the code for 'CHOCKS ARE IN PLACE'.

The smell of aviation fuel excited me! Thailand was just the same – "same but different" (common local sales pitch lingo). Thailand is the same but different alright! It's probably the only airport that I've visited where the guy riding a motor bike on the runway carries a shot gun over his shoulder, or where a terminal has kittens to play with and free sandwiches! Not that the new giant Suvarnabhumi Airport did, but many islands I've travelled to were very eccentric and, as mad as it sounds, it was just the best experience.

Cat cafés at airports could really catch on! Any entrepreneurs reading this? Free mocha on my tabby please ☺

Chapter 28

My father's house was about 2 hours south of Bangkok, in the Chonburi Country Province, rich with pineapple fields and endless coconut trees surrounding the crazy, sometimes smelly city of Pattaya, where Pete and Jade's café was to be! PETE N JADE's COFFEE SHOP.... Wow!

After selling our lives for a dream and leaving our home, dog and friends, the next few words out of Dad's mouth as he drove us from the airport came as quite a shock. "Actually, Son, there's been a slight change of plan.... I've bought a restaurant instead. The reason is...." he began to explain, but his next words were lost on me as my heart was sinking! In one moment, the visions I had of our little coffee shop had evaporated. By the look on Jade's face, she was obviously just as shocked, but surely, it was going to be ok! What did we know about restaurants? After locked-in syndrome, running a restaurant was probably not the best idea, not that my Dad saw it that way. He was running with an idea he thought would work – and, by God, we were lucky to be there at all!

Too tired to argue, I just wanted to get unpacked and settled for the night. The whole ordeal was emotionally draining. Months of planning, saying goodbye to all we had known for 7 years, leaving my Mum, sister, 2 cats and (most of all) Cody - who wouldn't understand. I was his (Cody's) best friend; we had hobbled and wobbled the roads together over every broken step.... "Stop this Pete, it's going to be fine!"

Dad and Noi showed us to our lovely little apartment above his office and our spirits lifted. It had been freshly painted with tiled floors and a little balcony overlooking the busy Thai street. Mopeds purred past while a mobile soup kitchen plied its trade below us.... noodle soup for a dollar per bowl! We wouldn't starve at that price!

How cool was this? Whooowhoooo! This was going to be awesome!!! We lived in Thailand!!!! From that moment, I felt free from the stroke.

The next morning Dad and Noi took us to our new restaurant, as excited to show it to us as we were to see it, having worked hard for months to get it ready. "Welcome to COCO's!"

No surprise to me; like all Dad and Noi's projects... this was CLASS! While not pissing in his pocket, I have to give them credit - they certainly had an eye for style. Big new windows, colour-coordinated with a flaming red and beach-yellow decor, strategically placed bright green cane palms in black pots, comfortable chairs on one side, black tables on the other, coffee counter with red bar stools, big stainless steel and red coffee machine; it was like something you'd see in a classy American downtown location with a hard-rock-meets-Starbucks-kinda-feel - a bar/coffee shop/restaurant/chillout zone, throughout. I have to say it was stunning to look at. Well done Dad and Noi!

"As much as this is blowing me away," I said to my Dad in my nasally voice, "... how can we run it?"

"Oh, don't worry," he replied airily, "You'll have staff running it with you."

Sitting down for breakfast we were just as staggered by the menu. Breakfast, lunch, evening meals - great choice, great value – and staff! This was way, WAY more than we bargained for. My dad has always been a grand thinker, a dreamer and this was one dream I wanted to share, truly I did. But after my past year, I was a shadow of my former self and still brain-damaged from the stroke; the very thought of this project was exhausting. What made things worse, I didn't know how to express my feelings.

Looking around at what had been achieved for us and I think for my dad too. Dad was obviously FULLY invested in his vision; nothing by halves for him! I guess I have that trait too, in many ways, but I was mentally smashed that year and this was all too overwhelming. My vision was of opening up a really simple place with just a few tables where Jade could get to know the regulars; one she could manage at a nice, easy pace - no pressure - while I could wash up, wipe tables, reload the coffee beans and be Jade's lackey. It wasn't about making money for me; I just wanted to get better and make Jade happy. Funny how you build castles in the sky. Dreams are often just that but, as always, despite my gratitude to Dad, I was thinking half full and the scale of this enterprise completely took me aback.

"Full breakfast, please." "*Khob khun krab*"....that's "Thank You" in Thai, which to me sounds like capon-un-crab. *Krab* is used when addressing a male, while for a female it's *ka*. Problem for me was that Thai is a tonal language so, when pronounced in my flat-toned, nasally voice, my words were meaningless! I WAS SCREWED!!! The language barrier was another thing I hadn't thought about back in Perth.

Lovely as they were and hard as they tried, Thai people simply couldn't understand me. Neither my English, nor my pigeon Thai, made any sense to listeners when channelled through my post-paralysis vocals! Even so, I made a fist of this new lingo, memorising numbers 1-10 and basic words like *tomorrow*, *later*, *please* and *thank you*. I also used compliments such as *beautiful* when I wanted to be charming, but also cracked jokey words like *tight arse* if appropriate – all stuff we'd picked up during our 6-month exile to Thailand after Australia kicked us out due to that bloody mix up with our visas!

Of course, you have to be careful with the Thai language as some words (like *beautiful*) have multiple meanings and if pronounced wrongly could easily be misinterpreted. This will spin you out! One perfect example is the English phrase "new wood doesn't burn". In Thai this is *mai mai mai mai* – just pronounced with different tones! You see my problem? With my poor

'Johnny-one-note' speech issues, Thailand was NOT the brightest of ideas after locked-in syndrome!

On arrival, there was a welcoming party for us, complete with friends and staff I knew from C.S.P. Construction waving as we pulled up, and a huge banner saying, "Welcome Home". Dad and Noi had really pushed the boat out for us and, looking back, I wish I could have embraced it all with more enthusiasm. Again, my speech let me down. Surrounded by so many people, I just couldn't make myself heard, which was awkward, especially as my great friend Paul was there and I really wanted to talk to him. We hadn't seen each other since I left Thailand a few weeks before my stroke. Nobody could appreciate that after the trauma I'd been through I just wanted to be in small, quiet company, so I could talk more easily. In loud places it was really hard to express myself at the time, as I could only utter two words per breath with any volume. No one had a clue how much it burned my lungs, causing even more fatigue in the process.

Writing this now in 2018, I feel a right 'whinging pom', but imagine running a 1000m long-distance event, times that by 1000, take away your voice, and add a body that's weak as piss, with sleeping issues, PTSD ,depression, fatigue and anxiety (to name but a few) and then be encircled by loads of people wanting to talk to you! It was all too much for me. Even so, I smiled as always, took the microphone and said: "Thank you all for making such an effort for Jade and me. It is so very kind of everyone. Thank you!" And I meant it!

That week there was to be a grand official opening for the restaurant. Determined to seem keen, most days since we had arrived we walked the 800m from our apartment to Coco's nice and early, to iron out any issues well in advance of the big event. A rail had been fitted to the apartment staircase, which certainly helped, and I enjoyed the walk, taking in the bustling atmosphere and weird, exotic smells of kitchen stalls preparing for the day's business at the side of the road. On the downside, walking was still hard. In that humidity, at 7.30am and with the odd, crazy dog with mite-infested sarcoptic mange, there were times Jade and I got snappy - that's putting it mildly! I'd learned to accept *soi* dogs (street dogs) but hated to see them go untreated. Sadly, I was unable to fix the dog problem – it was hard enough to fix myself! And we had one major road to deal with before making it to Coco's.

Sukhumvit, the one main road that runs right through the city of Pattaya, has 4 lanes crammed with mopeds humming like bees, trucks with impatient drivers and ear-splitting horns, taxi drivers clapping to attract attention of potential fares, and smells. Always smells. It was very daunting for me. I took Jade's hand like a child. Crossing the road was a nightmare, as Thai traffic lights are different because they operate a countdown system which shows how many seconds you have to get to the other side. Actually, I rather liked that part. What I didn't like, was the massive step onto the road. What I hated was the red light which encourages drivers to stop "IF YOU WANT TO"!!! I couldn't believe how many cars ignored this sign and ran the light minutes after it turned red. Pedestrians had to keep looking both ways while crossing, which was bloody frightening for us, particularly as I simply couldn't run! I needed that bloody coffee at COCO's on making it! Fortunately, Jade was a pro barista and her delicious concoctions settled my nerves.

Dad had very kindly given me a checklist. Number One, make sure there's always enough toilet paper and soap in the bathrooms. "Of course, YOU can't do that, because your visa has restrictions, but keep an eye on the staff, son." All well and good, but to some of the staff this is a totally new concept, as they don't have homes with bog rolls or soap dispensers. Toilet paper is not the norm in Asia, where citizens use a water hose instead and, if they're lucky, a pan with no handle in a bowl of water – the standard form of sanitation behind many a bar we've frequented!

A simple task for me, ey! Yeah, right! In Thailand, nothing is simple. I don't mean that with any disrespect; it's just so hard for me, what with the language, and the fact that our culture and thinking are completely different makes it a real challenge. Here's me asking a young girl to do something I could easily have done myself, had I been legally allowed. All I could do was point to a soap dispenser and say, *"Dem tang, kab"* ("Fill up, please.") Whether I wasn't pronouncing it correctly, or my voice just wasn't tonal enough, the poor girl had no idea what I was trying to tell her; she didn't know what liquid soap was and neither of us knew where it was kept. Eventually, I did the logical thing and went to buy some at the 7 Eleven store next door where, unable to find any liquid soap on the shelves and still struggling to make myself understood, I resorted to hand-pump actions to the lady behind the till! Looking back, it seems quite funny now, but was very frustrating at the time.

I don't want to bang on about it, but things like that happened every day and I got so stressed trying to do right by my Dad that I decided they were best left to Noi, who spoke 5 languages: Lao (Isan Thai), Thai, Chinese, English and now Russian, due to the massive Russian migration.

Yep, there was little I could do apart from chatting to the ex-pats, limping from table to table. "Everything okay with your meal, sir?" After a while, I felt I was just invading their space and, although a few customers enjoyed my company at breakfast, most struggled to understand me – I probably gave them indigestion!

Legally, we couldn't serve people, wash up, take orders, set tables or even lift a cup and both me and Jade were driven crazy. Not being allowed to do anything directly and with staff who simply couldn't understand us, this venture was never going to work. Try as we might, we quickly realised that not only had the coffee shop dream disappeared, but with it any chance of us working together.

Bless my Dad for this fantastic looking place, and it's not that I wasn't grateful, but I was a worker, always have been. Okay, I couldn't do things quickly but even small tasks, like moving a plate or washing up, would at least have been a challenge and would have given me some purpose. In fact, after becoming independent, which (thank God) I had become to a degree, I believe 'purpose' is one of the most under-appreciated values of life and, along with being my own man again, it was something I craved.

In fact, I wanted it all – everything I'd lost – a goal I'm sure will resonate with other strokies. Purpose – Wow! What a prize! Yet so few people understand its importance until it's gone. When I talked to my dad about it he was very understanding. "Look Son, you don't have to be there all day, you know." So we tried to go home at lunch time. Working 4-5 hours for me was max, after that I needed a rest. As every stroke survivor knows, there's a point where you just crash and burn, you stop functioning properly and speech is gone!

Then came the phone calls. Noi: "Jade, what are you doing? Can you come to the restaurant now, please?" Then in the evening it was Dad: "Hi Peter, there's someone in the restaurant I'd like you meet." By this time I was mad with tiredness; I had no sleeping pills and the insomnia was unrelenting. Lack of sleep was used to torture prisoners in wartime, so I believe, and I can absolutely see why!

This hurts me to say, but I was literally going mental with it. Both Jade and I were tired, unsettled, missing our home and our animals. My sister Vicky was like Jade's sister too. Just everything! In Thailand we had no time to settle in and we were always on top of each other, getting in each other's way. The mojo wasn't right, we became cranky with each other and the worse our life became, the more our relationship suffered!

Had I only been the person I am today, I could have seen so clearly, and it would all be so different now. But hey, that's life! You can't change a damn thing; all you can do is grow from what life throws at you, but when you're living it you just can't see where it's going to end. After a stroke you don't even know if it WILL end.

Unbelievably, only months before our wedding our relationship was disintegrating. Friends were coming from across the world: Mum, Vicky, Sue, Ted, Julia, Matt, Gavin, Cousin Amanda, Leroy, Soda, Boyd, Dave, Sean, Eleanor, Alf - all from Oz; Pete, Danny and Andrea from the UK; Mark and Jackie, John and Elaine from New Zealand…. Oh, I can't mention everyone, much as I'd like to – it takes real friends to travel miles to a wedding overseas, yet the pressure was mounting. Not that I had doubts or anything, I just wasn't in the best head space to think about such things.

I don't think love was part of our relationship by then; did we even have a relationship at that point? I hadn't kissed or put my arm around Jade for longer than I remember, mainly due to my physical restrictions. Often, I wanted to just run my fingers through her hair and kiss her with meaning like I once did, but the stroke had changed me that way. The affectionate displays most couples take for granted were not easy for me, not that we ever got much time alone together when I wasn't exhausted.

After a couple of months in Thailand, Jade and Noi cooked a lovely dinner but I spoiled the evening by breaking down. I just lost it, cracked, realising I just couldn't go on.

"Son, whatever's the matter?" said Dad.

"I just can't do this…. It's all too much!"

"Why, Son?" I didn't say everything that was in my head at the time; about the roads that terrified me, having to hold Jade's hand like a child, the language barrier, the lack of sleep and the constant phone calls! Nor about my concern for Jade; who was also used to being her own boss with a car, a drink at night, phone calls to England, regular downtime, food and shops and habits. Everything in my life just felt wrong. I'd had enough of smiling and pretending I was strong. I was weak and just wanted to go home, yet 'home' was a memory, sold away. There was no fixing what I'd done to us!

Dad and Noi were so disturbed by the way we felt, so lost and unable to help. They'd tried to think for and plan everything for us, but it was just not Home! "What is it you want, Peter? Please help me understand!" I could tell Dad was hurt. The problem was that no normal person could understand what I said next.

"Dad, for so long I haven't had any time just to do normal things like lie on a sofa with my woman, just watching a film together, cuddling, just having some downtime together!" I'm not a soft guy but let me tell you this, when you can't move your body to kiss someone, when it's taken away by lack of muscle, you suffer. The simple pleasure of spooning with the person you love is worth millions!

But, sadly, my Dad wouldn't or couldn't understand. In fairness, I don't think he meant his words to come out quite as they did; I guess he was trying to be wise and fatherly: "Listen to me, Son. You can't spend your life cuddling on a sofa. You'll never be a millionaire or get anywhere in life, believe me Son." I'm sure if he reads this he'll say that's not what he meant, but I remember thinking, "I don't wanna be a f***ing millionaire. I just want to be held and hold someone again in my life!" I just cried and cried.

My Dad's always tried to bring me up to be a hard worker and my folks sure did an awesome job. What he said was to motivate me, I'm sure, but at that moment I realised I saw the world differently than most people. I'd changed from a happy-go-lucky, outgoing guy into quite an introvert.

Chapter 29

I'm glad we had that breakdown that night. Even if we failed to connect emotionally, at least we'd been honest about how we felt. Being open has always been my strongest asset and has stopped me from drowning many times. The fact that it wasn't working this time, nor was ever going to work, made one thing blisteringly clear to my father and Noi; Jade and I had to go back to Australia. Fortunately, they understood, but it must have been a painful pill to swallow.

Next morning, Dad and I met up at Coco's. "These things happen in life." Dad took a sip of his coffee and sighed. "Perhaps we should have kept things simpler, so for that I'm sorry, Son. At least you gave it a go."

The anxiety left us both that day - the pressure was off, and I can only be grateful to Dad and Noi for the opportunity they offered. But, at that early stage of recovery from locked-in syndrome, running a busy restaurant was ridiculous.

Life in Thailand for the next remaining few months was still very tricky; although we were no longer tied to Coco's and the staff ran things Thai style, with total efficiency. I always felt like a Ronald MacDonald statue anyway, standing there greeting people with a stupid grin was all I could do on my visa.

That chapter of my life over, our wedding now became the focus, consuming most of our energies, particularly as the small garden wedding we'd first planned had somehow moved to a hotel on the glamorous Royong Beach – courtesy of my great Dad and Noi, whose wedding gift to us was the wedding itself. Naturally, I was grateful, not having a pot to piss in, as they say (diddly squat!). Not being used to hand-outs, it really hurt my pride, yet my hands were tied and we accepted gracefully.

That being said, wedding plans were very much taken away from us and although I think Jade would have liked to organise her own big day herself, we didn't have a thing - not a penny or a contact – leaving us cap in hand as usual. It's a horrible feeling to rely so completely on somebody else but, with it being my Dad, I could just about swallow it and actually feel blessed with it all.

A few things were left to us. I got myself a tailor-made suit while Jade had bought her dress from Perth 6 months earlier and with all the arrangements in hand, Dad and Noi were determined to make the remainder of our stay in Thailand as much fun as possible. Weeks before our friends arrived, we had a few nights in Bangkok, where one of the highlights was a Fawlty Towers performance in a restaurant where dinner was served by the whole cast! Absolute MADNESS, but OMG it was bloody hilarious. 'Basil Fawlty' was marching around messing table orders up, 'Manuel' getting his head-slapped for dropping the bread, and 'Sybil' yelling at 'Basil' like she tended to do! At one point, everyone had to go outside while they tried to kill a rat Manuel spotted under the tables! It was just fantastic! I never got to eat my steak from laughing, the rarest steak I'll ever have for sure! Just a truly magical night that really took away the stress of the Coco's fiasco.

Not much else that I remember gave me sore guts in that whole year, I can tell ya, but, "Oh Mr Fawlty... Mr Fawlty! I, A RAT!!!" Under tables, on the tables, everyone's faces.... And what made it even funnier was the Thai diners there who'd never been subjected to the likes of Fawlty Towers and were actually frightened, I think; which I'm ashamed to say, just made it even more hilarious – especially as Thai people are so gentle. I was unable to breathe, literally struggling to take a breath from hysteria! Never in my life have I laughed so hard.

I hate Bangkok by day but at night it comes alive and is just amazing. One evening, we had a Black Russian in the Moon Bar on the roof of the highest building in Bangkok, which overlooked the entire city. The height was ridiculous and, although a lift carries guests 95% of the way, climbing the spiral stairs to the top was bloody hard work for me and very scary too. But me being me, I just had to try and can now say with confidence I am (probably) the only locked-in survivor to have climbed them. As for the view...WOW! You've got to see it!

The fact that I couldn't move at the top, we will not shout about; enough to say that the thought of walking back down again sent my legs, already rigid with fear, into spasm. "What a tit!" Memories of that experience gave me the shits for years - very dangerous too!

I first started using escalators in Thailand, holding Jade's hand! It was really the most frightening thing to me, trying to keep my balance, then trying to get the timing right to get on and off. Such a morbid fear of falling is something 99% of people – even some with disabilities - wouldn't or couldn't even imagine. I say this because it's true, yet can appreciate how many people reading would just love to be given the same chance, and to them I apologise; I can only write my story from my perspective.

Surprisingly I am not going to talk much about our amazing wedding in Thailand, although I intended to. I'll go as far as to say it was a very special gift and a memory I'll always remember, but my stroke took away the glitter - and believe me, there was plenty of glitter, thanks to my brilliant Dad and Noi who were so very, very kind.

Saying 'I do' in my nasally post-stroke voice was massively special, after what we had faced over the previous months. Yet exchanging vows almost didn't take place due to flooding in Pataya; when water 3m high almost stopped the celebrant from arriving until at least an hour after the ceremony should have begun. I tried to view the storm as a blessing (maybe it was!) and, to everyone's relief, it ceased as soon as Jade and I were legally hitched. Foolishly, I thought that would be the end of storms in my life. Little did I know!

Many people won't understand why I choose to fast forward now, but I feel I have that right, having been open all the way so far. Somehow, I didn't feel this was a story book wedding; rather, I appreciated the magnitude of what it took to actually stand there. From trying to control my pee and blinking out the letters "I will get back to you!" on my word board, to saying "I do!" in front of friends and family, certainly merits some recognition as weddings go!

I also appreciate how many people travelled great distances for the occasion and hope everyone enjoyed it as much I did, seeing them there is a forever memory! Thank you all so much for making it such a magical night! Highlights can be viewed on my online video page, including a comic rendition of 'Perfect Day' filmed by Dad's friend Martin.

Chapter 30

BING BONG....FLIGHTS FOR PERTH WESTERN AUSTRALIA!

I skipped a lot of detail in the last chapter and am sorry for that. The whole adventure was clouded somewhat by a stupid argument on the day we left; private family stuff, discussed via mobile while looking out of a cheap hotel window before ending in heartfelt apologies. "I'm sorry, Son!" "I'm sorry too, Dad!"

I looked at all the corrugated shacks below my window, unable to believe I was crying while people were literally showering below me in the open. It seemed clear to me that we're all living in hell, just in different ways, and if you don't understand what I'm saying then I guess you've been lucky so far.

Yes... to the gate, 3 miles away! This airport was a city of travellators. We didn't talk much, Jade and I, both of us lost in a sea of emotions during this trip, which had thrown up many issues we hadn't even thought of before coming to Thailand!

Leaving, I felt like a dog coming home with my tail between my legs, only I no longer had a home; no home, no garden, no car, no jobs, no Cody, no remnants of our previous life - just three cases containing the remains of our possessions. But good old Mum was there! She had, of course, seen us at the wedding and knew things just weren't right, as did our friends who also picked up on our negative vibes! Why was it that everyone else could see what I couldn't? The fact I couldn't answer this question made me feel more stupid than ever!

And what a miserable start to our married life, living with your Mum in a single room, broke, and broken. Musing on these sorrows made our flight to Perth the longest 9 hours! Staring at the clouds below me I was trying to think of what was to become of us now. No matter what anyone could say, I was the biggest failure. I was sunk!

I was never so happy to hear those damn crows at Perth airport, their raucous cawing, grating to the ears, was now telling me "You're safe now, Pete!" WAAK.... WAAK .... WAAAAAAARK - in that moaning tone, as if to say "GOD!!! DO I HAVE TO?" in an almost depressing, last breath tone!

At that moment outside Perth's small supermarket sized airport, I knew where my heart lay: "Home'!!!!!! WESTERN AUSTRALIA. I was a fair dinkum Aussie, a seed firmly planted in the sun-baked soil.

WA, often known as Wait Awhile on account of being a bit behind on certain things, was where I belonged, and the vast blue, open skies spoke to me that day, reminding me of something I'd read over a decade before. Western Australia was: "A land where anybody can fight their way to the top." That's all I had now, words. I clung onto that phrase for the next four years, from that day amongst the crows at Arrivals 'Pay n Display'.

Chapter 31

Alexander Heights, overlooking the surrounding suburbs, was pretty cool. From here you could see all the palm trees that pommie immigrants had planted over the years, as these newcomers found their own roots in this wonderful sunny new world. Today, Perth is like a little Britain, where you're always hearing different accents from the Motherland (as well as other countries), making for a vibrant, multicultural melting pot which has yet to catch up with eastern capitals. Wait Awhile - ha-ha.

As for the views…. you can see for miles! Bush fires bellowing smoke that would make most people panic are the norm here, where burn-offs are a regular feature. Bush or scrub ground cover, such as gum leaves, is deliberately set alight (in a controlled way) by fire fighters, making it less easy to fuel a possible fire from lightning strikes or some arsehole who wants to kill everyone with a discarded cigarette. Fires can be bloody frightening for country folk; we witnessed a massive fire which got out of control in the Perth hills one year, glowing red all night, with ash flakes falling on car driveways 20kms away.

The first few months I lived there was a reflective time for me. I spent many an hour patio staring, you know, when you just stare at things in deep, dark thoughts. Good job we had a nice view!

Trooper as she is, Jade found herself a job, jumping straight into café work to support us both. We were penniless and I felt ashamed about absolutely everything!

As for Mum, she got all Mum on me, telling me to put it all behind me and move forward. We all try to do this, of course, but not after locked-in syndrome, you numpty! LOL! But she was right, of course. I needed to stop feeling sorry for myself. It wasn't helping.

My mate Dan De Silva popped around one morning to cheer me up. He was at my wedding, having been sent to Asia on business by his company.

"Pete what can you do these days?" he asked. I looked at him blankly. "What do you mean?" "Well," he replied, "I think we can find you some things to do at my company- Anapurna. I've a welder called Glen who might pick you up on the way through. Meantime, get yourself some boots!" Then off he went in his new convertible, leaving me with a big grin!

"Mum! Guess what? Dan's gonna get me a job in his factory! A real job! All I need are steel toe-cap work boots!!!" Jade was the next to be told when she arrived home from the café and her sense of relief was tangible. "That'll be a great help, I'm sure!" OMG, I thought! Once the euphoria died down I started getting anxiety big time. "Was I ready?"

My voice was still much the same as it was on my first online video, although I could say more words per sentence (about four) before running out of puff, my right hand and arm were very limited, my leg was stiff as a plank and I was actually scared. But I was ready!

That week I heard a man say something on TV that helped me for that whole year! He said: "Anxiety is sometimes mixed up emotions. Anxiety is almost the same feeling as excitement." He said it again. "Anxiety is almost exactly the same feeling as excitement. So next time anxiety comes over you, tell yourself over and over you're excited ... smile ... you're excited... this could be amazing!!!" That actually worked for me in a way.

The following week, at 5.30am in the pitch dark, I'm flapping my arms at the bus stop on Alexander Drive; an exercise I use to try to increase movement when I'm alone. I wasn't getting the bus, but it was a good pick up point.

I was waiting for Big Glen. 6'1" in his stockinged feet and solid with it, Big Glen was aptly named. In fact, as I watched him smashing slag off welds in the workshop, he reminded me of Thor, only more Gerald Butler looking, which was the most distinctive thing about him. The 45-

minute drive to work was all it took to get to know him. I got to know he didn't talk much!

At first I thought it was me. My job was to empty bins and be his lackey in the corner of the workshop, which I found extremely uncomfortable. Nobody spoke, not even at 'smoko' (an Aussie term for lunch) when everyone sat munching their sandwiches in total silence, or speaking into their mobiles to avoid talking to their colleagues. This was a far cry from my building days when we all swore at each other, broke wind, bantered and wound each other up…. you know, stupid crap like, who's Mum we'd taken out. But at Anapurna, not a word!

Being paranoid, I more or less decided I wouldn't be coming back the next day when… someone spoke to me! "So what happened to you, then?" Not "where do you live?" or, "what did you do before?" Just straight to it. I replied in this Darth Vader voice: "I had brain stem stroke a couple of years ago." "Shit!" he said. "F***ed you up, ey!" Then he looked back at his phone! That was it, my one conversation of the day!!!

Anapurna was an aluminium and steel fabricators that supplied and delivered state wide but has since closed down, I believe. They did everything from steel brackets on a massive scale to hold-together concrete tilt-up panels (or concrete walls to anybody else) for industrial units or factories.

All day long, there were countless drills whining, flashes of welding which I had to look away from, big steel cutting saws, drill presses and CNC (computer numerical control) machines, giant computer routers etching plastic into hard to visualise shapes! It was bloody noisy, I tell ya - perfect for people with speech and hearing problems!

I already had a hearing deficit, caused years ago by two guys on my 457 visa blowing my right eardrum, so without ear defenders it was sheer agony. I suffered with tinnitus too and speaking was a nightmare, reducing me to the odd shake or nod of my head, which was not going to help my speech – in fact, I realised this would set me back considerably.

One of my jobs was drilling holes, sometimes all day, drilling into steel which squealed like a pig when it needed oiling, while the drill bit would jam and break at regular intervals. This was my life at Anapurna.

To his credit, Glenn tried to find me other jobs like spraying the odd bracket with fire retardant or finding a certain sized screw. Easy enough, but I was so bored, I started moaning and screaming at the same pitch as the noise in the factory!

Arrhhhhhhhhhhhhhhhhhhhhhhhhhh
Arrrhhhhhhhhhhhhhhhhhhhhhhhhhhhh
Arhhhhhhhhhhhhhhhhhhhhhhhhhhhh

Thinking about it, this was the same exercise my speechy David Harrison had encouraged me to do in Shents. Unfortunately, my breath support was so pathetic I found it impossible. The best I could manage back then was 3-4 seconds.

Pretty much most days I was given hundreds of steel brackets to drill - 3 holes x 3 in every side. This could have been tricky, yet with the help of a punch maker I couldn't really mess up. All I had to do was keep drilling while standing and go "Arrrrrhhhhhhhhhhhhhhhh Arhhhhhhhhhhhhhhh." Change bracket... drill... 9 holes in 10 minutes(ish)... whoowhoooo! Gripping stuff! To make life more interesting, I'd try changing my tone by yodelling, which didn't really work, except occasionally when I screamed.

On the plus side, after the first month or so the guys started warming to me and their command to "empty the bins" or whatever, now came with a "please, Pete." Then, once I'd completed the task, extra words were added such as "Good lad!" or "Good on ya, buddy!" A few lads even started looking at me when they talked to Glenn, including me in the conversation. And the foreman Boyd knew someone with locked-in syndrome so he was on the level. I was becoming a factory mascot I guess!

Though the actual work was tedious, I eventually got to work alongside everyone, becoming part of the team and gaining confidence. Sometimes the drill bit got stuck in the steel then spun round and banged my fingers so hard I wanted to sit down. Most people jump around screaming, but I just sat feeling sick to stomach with the pain; took my skin off a couple of times... blood everywhere! Funny how things work out! I actually hated that job but I know now it was the making of me - and not just because of the finger-fine motor skills I was developing; something happened at Anapurna that to this day gets me emotional. I am crying again now... Bloody soft arse, ey!

This is how I remember it! While operating the drill press, I was singing any old crap to myself, and then I started chanting the old football anthem: OLAY, OLAY, OLAY, OLAY... OLAY... OLAY!!! My voice had started to break!!!

Chapter 32

Glen wasn't at Anapurna for long but he was awesome to work with, lifting the steel I couldn't lift and trying to keep me away from the bin job. Sometimes I'd drop the bins in the skip because my fingers couldn't grasp the bin handle - really pissed me off, did that.

Glen also helped me get driving again by selling me his car, which I loved; a Commodore, a real Aussie classic. Jade had taken me to the independent living centre (ILC), where they help you with absolutely everything from around the house aids to modifying cars to suit your needs and offering driving lessons for people like me. So I was already thinking about getting back into the driver's seat of my life in every sense!

I was extremely lucky, as during my fight back I'd managed to win a lot of my body. My own obsessive behaviour had got me so far, as you have read, so for me only a left-hand accelerator pedal was needed – oh, and a ball for the steering wheel – for my first few lessons. I'd already passed the visual simulator test, where you have to describe everything you see as the car drives and was used to the clock way of explaining: "Mum with pram left side waiting, at 11 o'clock!" "Kid on bike 500 meters ahead on the right, 10 o'clock!" "Blah, blah, blah." Well, we had to make sure I wasn't going to kill anyone, of course!

The thought of Glen's car was incredible! I'd no money but asked Dave for a loan, should I pass the test. Luckily I had full peripheral vision (60 degree left and right), which certainly helped. My heart bleeds for some of my strokie friends who have lost their vision – like my mate Craig. Dr Watts we called him in Shents - a name which has stuck. He was always checking on me to see I was okay, telling the nurses if I'd been to the toilet and what I'd eaten. Craig was my voice, bless him! Sadly, he wasn't able to regain driving, but he's doing okay in his own little place now and I still pop in every few months to make pizza and watch net flicks. "You need to walk more," I keep telling him, but he's happy, I think.

Olay, Olay, Olay, Olay... Olay... Olay!

I only worked about 3 days a week - good job too! My insomnia at that time was by far the worst in my battle back to health; sometimes going 3 nights with hardly any sleep! Honestly, these were dangerous times. Work and driving lessons; I was struggling to deal with life, just existing as a zombie, walking like one too! I'd come home from that aluminium factory in rags and all I wanted was to sit with Jade and eat dinner on the sofa in front of the TV. Too tired to talk but wanting to, same as any bloke would!

Jade and my Mum were very close - almost like a mother and daughter - so a lot of times the two of them would be drinking wine on the patio, chatting away. It was clear Jade needed that; her life was nothing like it had been. Neither was I, she said. That still hurts me now. We strokies or ABIs often compared notes about such comments as, "the day I loss my man," or "he's different now!"

Well I guess we are, but I wasn't in my head. I was suffering with a body that doesn't move the same, a voice that wouldn't come out the same and I didn't want to get pissed or smoke anymore! Can't think why? I was lonely and needed comfort and attention. I felt ugly and needed reassurance, companionship and my best friend.

To me, I was still the Pete I was in my head - still am today - but no. I sat on the sofa, night after night while the girls talked away on the patio! Reluctantly, I tried to sit with them, catching the odd smoke drift. Although I didn't want to sit outside after a 5.30am start I needed to be with someone. Time after time, I somehow got into arguments, eventually getting so angry I wanted my own place but couldn't afford it Arrrrrrrrrrrrrrrrrrrrrrrrrrrrrhh.

Every day these frustrations made me angry and ever more determined I was going to get back my life. MY WAY! This was doing my head in; staring at my drilling brackets in despair, losing concentration now and then, paying the price badly if the bit got jammed. OUCH, the pain!!

Olay, olay, olay, olay...........

Oh God why? Why is this life so shit?!!!!! To be honest, I didn't see how my life could get better; I felt that way every damn day of this bastard stroke! I have the right to swear!!! I will not excuse myself, sorry!

Chapter 33

Working at Anapurna was hard, but there were compensations... such as Brett. One day, he walked in, an Aussie Eminem, pants hanging off, full of tatts, huge beard - I swear he was ready for a rap battle!

Brett introduced himself: "Hey Bro! What's happening? I'm Brett, the new welder!"

He didn't seem to notice my lack of movement. "You had a stroke Bro? Damn, that's f*** up!" He was never one to mince his words.

Straightaway I liked him. "What's this shit?" Snorting with disgust, he turned off the radio, replacing it with speakers attached to his phone. Next thing, the darkest rap was blastin'! F*in' this, f*in' that - totally not the norm for the factory, but I liked his crazy vibe.

In my world crazy music just seemed to fit, although the dark lyrics were a little disturbing to Gonz, judging by his face! Such a picture! Gonz came from Peru, South America and was a great bloke, always looking out for me, telling me what cereals had the most protein, or what exercises I should do!

So, with his cigarettes and this crazy shit Brett was playing, I don't think Gonz liked him at first, but we all warmed to his crazy personality and the mad stuff he'd create. Brett could weld absolutely anything - tools, cigarette boxes, jewellery boxes... ANYTHING! He let me try a bit of welding myself, nothing comparable to him, of course, but I became brave enough to hold a grinder, grinding the slag off the welds. That was stupid, I know. I could have taken my fingers off, but I tell you what - I held that grinder as hard as I could, another exercise that strengthened my grip. My job was proving to be the best rehab!

There was a massive metal-cutting machine in our rap blasting corner. Sometimes the blade would take 5-15 mins to cut through the steel – I spent months watching that blade, making sure water kept flowing on it to keep it cool. Brett knew I liked that job. He saw that I had made myself two little weights out of the cut steel and taped them up with masking tape. I would hold them out from my hips only about 30-50cm, an exercise that burned after a few minutes (Arrrrhhh!), taking comfort in the angry rap, fighting the burn daily and managing to lift them higher and higher.

You can kind of get a picture of why I was so messed up at that time of my life; daily factory life was like the gym for me where I spent 6 hours a day, 3 days a week. Looking back, I'm convinced the job was sent to me, providing the perfect physiotherapy with an income and Eminem's music thrown in! I may not go to church, but I'm open to higher guidance, something you don't see until you look back – in my case six years later.

All I know is crazy welder Brett was sent to me just when I needed him and we're still in contact today. Sad to say, he's now fighting his own battles – I am sorry to say with multiple scleroses (MS). I sometimes wonder why we're all here. Is it just to learn about pain, loss, and suffering, with a bit of love thrown in if you're lucky?

Maybe I was sent to him too, as I understand what he's talking about on the phone. In a strange way, I feel Brett's battle has been kind of tailor-made for him, as he's now helping everyone at the MS centre, cheering everyone up as he once did me and making the girls smile. He tells me girls go crazy for his beard, although I'm not too sure about that! Yet it's good to hear my mate's giving them some old chat! Thanks for the 'rap corner' of smoke 'n' flashes Bro! It really helped me.

Skipping forward now to what Aussies often refer to as a lobotomy! Yes - you know - a surgical operation to the prefrontal lobe of the brain; otherwise known fondly as Aussie citizenship! I was in for the op on the 26th January, 2013, one of my proudest years.

500 hundred people of all nationalities gathered that sunny morning at Wanneroo Show Grounds. Like most events over here, sizzling smells wafted through the

air while 50-odd people queued patiently for free sausage and onion hotdogs – a great start to their new lives as Aussies! Some people I know waited 5-8 years for the application to go through. As for me, my visa took 5 years and thousands of failed applications. But today wasn't a day to complain about the immigration system. Today was magical and as Aussie as you could get! As jet planes performed fly-bys above (which always gives me a rush), we entered a giant tent accompanied by the famous song 'We come from a land down under'. Inside, a huge cardboard kangaroo smiled down at us from the stage and there were 500 chairs, each sporting little Aussie flags and gifts for every occupant.

Looking around at my fellow citizens, I realised I wasn't the only one who'd been through hell to get here! Australia has a large intake of asylum seekers from war-torn countries, for whom this was an emotional end to their horrible ordeals. That day gave me the promise of a new future, to live and work in a safe, warm land with law and order and customs I felt protected by, and which, hopefully, others wanted to learn and live by too.

Wanneroo's Mayor, looking magnificent, her gold chain of office glinting in the light, began her speech by acknowledging the Nyoongar people's sacred ground of Wanneroo - ('Wanna' meaning digging stick used by Aboriginal women, and 'Roo' meaning place).

Aboriginal culture is now greatly respected, as history unfolds the secrets which shape this great land with its never-ending, mind-boggling space. Did you know the entire UK could fit into Australia 31.28 times!

The ceremony then continued with speakers who had faced adversity, people who'd lost limbs or loved ones, or seen their families torn apart through tragedy – stories that have stayed with me to this day, emotionally distressing yet somehow bonding us all together.

A lot of people fear immigration, because customs and belief systems don't always allow for integration, but I like to think it's our differences that make a country great. Diversity brings choice, foods, fashions and general influences. So when I looked into people's eyes that day, I didn't see or feel any sense of segregation, I saw 500 people united by hope and dreams of tomorrow.

Finally, we all stood for the national anthem 'Advance Australia Fair' followed by 500 waving flags, tears all round (especially from yours truly!) and a host of emotions I can't even describe, as the jets flew over once again. I'd been officially 'lobotomised'! The deed now done, I hobbled off to start life with my frontal lobe dead set on the future... and a piss in the billabong (that's Aussie slang for a can of beer in the pool!)

Yes, my inauguration was a great day, but all the excitement sapped the life out of me. As happened so often, my lack of energy had ruined the day for Jade. I was as irritating as an old mobile phone having to be plugged in every 3-4 hours – all I wanted was to recharge my batteries.

In fact, the whole year was complete overload for me. And, yes, I lost my job at the factory. "Last in first out," I was told. "We're gearing up to move overseas, you see, Pete. Sorry mate." And that was it. Still, I had taken a lot from that place; improved speech, fine-tuned motor skills, confidence and, oh, not to forget, I bleed a lot when hit with steel spinning brackets!

Chapter 34

Losing that job deflated me a bit, but it made me start walking again. And my mate Duncan got me a part-time cleaning job at a plastics supplier, so that was something!

"Pete, if you get registered self-employed you can clean the offices, every Saturday mate!"

"Nice one, Duncan!"

There were 3 offices, 2 toilets and a kitchen. A pretty simple job for me: mopping, hoovering, emptying bins and cleaning toilets, except I took 3 hours to do it and only got paid for 2 hours, because that's what an average person would take. Anyway, I stuck at it and a few years later got the job done in 1 hour 30 minutes... quite a record! At least now, I'm getting my time back!

Seems like I've been cleaning toilets on and off my whole life; from cleaning clubs in Manchester, with my uncle Eddie, to scrubs in the army every morning before breakfast! If the N.C.Os found one pubic hair you were on toilet duty every night too! Either that or guard duty and trust me, you would choose toilets every time - military police can run you ragged!

By the time I started the new job, I was walking a few kilometres a week. My drop foot still caught me out occasionally, but I wasn't falling nearly as much, once a month maybe, and decided to register for a major challenge.

Perth's biggest running and walking event, the great 'City to Surf' was held every year with a choice of distance. For about $50 (can't remember the exact fee) I put myself down for the 12km.

"12km!!" Jade and Mum were a little concerned as usual – and I don't think Jade was especially keen on a 12km walk at the weekend, after working all week! But I was hell bent on it. This was a focus I needed!

Up until then, 7km was the most I'd done, which included at least an hour break before heading back home, so 12km with hills, no benches, and no break at all was a little scary.

Maybe I hoped my neurologist, Professor David Blacker would advise me against it on medical grounds! His email in response said quite the opposite! "That's fantastic, Pete! Do you want me to walk with you?" Well, if you're going to do something stupid like a marathon hike, it helps to have a top medical personal consultant by your side! How many professors do that, ey? What a legend!

All I could do when David first met me after my locked-in stroke was move my head around the bed as if to say, "Pick me! Pick me!" as he decided which patients to take from post I.C.U.

Now he'd offered to walk with me, giving me more of a motive than ever. Not wanting to let him down, I got totally obsessed in the weeks leading up, even to the point where I had blisters from walking, which sometimes popped; that was a disgusting feeling!

My foot wasn't landing right when I walked, causing my toes, that could hardly move, to rub and rub against one another.

City to Surf 2013: Locked-in survivor attempts 12km walk! The pressure was on... I think I was the only man in the history of the event to enter with locked-in syndrome! My number was 32176, my trainers were new, and I was standing at the station with hundreds of other people, waiting for the city-bound train.

Perth simply blew me away! There were literally thousands who'd entered - 48,000 I believe – and never in my life had I taken part in any big event. Truth is, the old me would probably have thought, "Stuff that!"

But today, I was glad I'd entered. Being one of 48,000 people all reaching for a goal was electrifying, it really was! If you want a flavour of my excitement that day, you can watch my interview on my website petercoghlan.com or on YouTube. Actually, I felt the video wasn't really good P.R. for the event and for that I felt bad, but let me tell it how it was....

As Jade and I met Professor Blacker, the Stroke Foundation lady (Jonine Collins) was taking pictures to inspire others on their newsfeed. All the time I was thinking to myself, "You've done it now, Pete! Everyone's watching you. You have to do this!"

I thought of all the strokies and people with acquired brain injuries out there who might read or see the post. I was going to do this or die in the attempt, damn it! To help people believe in a different tomorrow. This was my big chance to lead others for once in my life. I'd never been a leader - I was always the one nobody wanted when picking football teams in school, but now I felt this was my moment to prove myself.

The moment had come. We all moved to the start line with our bib numbers and waited for that air horn, 2 mins to go - check laces, adjust cap, apply sunscreen, stretch my calves... pathetically! But I was there and I had the fire in my soul to complete it. "Please God, I don't want to fail everyone!" Not just fellow strokies, but a lot of people who'd sponsored me too!

With an almighty honk, we were off! 47,999 people passed me in the first 20 minutes, but I expected that!

I was the only LIS veteran there, sporting my specially printed T-shirt emblazed with 'Stroke Survivor', so people could see why I was such a turtle.

Within an hour there was nobody to see, everyone had disappeared into the ether, leaving me to limp awkwardly several hours behind. My new trainers were not a good idea. Just 2km into the race I had to sit down, take off the fancy walkers and assess the damage.

Yep! You can't beat a massive blister full of fluid on a 12km walk with another 10km to go! Bloody hell! What a shit! I adjusted my socks, tied my laces even tighter to stop any movement and flicked my iPod to an epic score to help me dig deep to forget the pain.

For most of the way, Jade and David walked ahead of me, as I needed to concentrate on every step. I was still very much a falls risk on a kamikaze mission. I literally didn't care if I crashed. This was a personal goal to find out just how much I could take.

If someone asked you, how far can you walk? What would you say? I bet 99.9 % of people reading this who are able to walk couldn't answer that question. I HAD to know. The endless kilometres I'd walked that year, along with hydro and gym left me wondering too. Today I would find out.

At this stage, speed was not an issue. All I remember is, I was so bloody slow David had time to stop at the last coffee shop, wait for his order then catch me up, slurping his fix as he passed me by!

Hours passed, water stop after water stop, empty cups everywhere, as people didn't want to queue for a bin. With 48,000 cups at every stop, the road was a sea of white polystyrene crunching under my feet.

6km in, I felt my blister pop!

Chapter 35

6km and nobody around - no traffic, no people - and I realised the water stops were also packing up! This was a good sign, I thought, maybe we only had an hour left to go!

2 hours later, there wasn't a water station in sight, and all the people strategically placed to guide walkers had disappeared. Had my trusty Professor David not been familiar with the City to Surf I'd have been lost for sure!

There's a long road that stretches steeply down towards the ocean called Oceanic Drive (I think), but by the time I reached the top I was just too tired to notice the sign. My legs were getting very weak, as only someone with dodgy quadriceps would understand. It was really hard for me to lock my knees back into place, and my hips were just as shaky.

"Keep going, Pete!" urged David, "we're really close now!" Now as any whinging Pom will tell you, an Aussie's idea of 'close' can mean anything from 5 to 50km!

A case in point. When laying bricks one ridiculously hot day in the hills of Mundaring, I was gasping for a drink and turned to my colleague. "Sorry Graham, I just gotta go to a shop because I've finished the 3 litres I brought!" Yes! 3 bloody litres, that's how crazy hot a day on the bricks in WA can be!

"Oh yeah, Mate - the shop's just down the road!" Now, for anyone unacquainted with the lingo, 'Just down the road' is Aussie-speak for a 6km hike! So David's reassuring, "Not far now, Pete!" was taken with a pinch of salt... another essential in this climate!

Some of the roads were quite dangerous, particularly those through bushland which fell away into 30 DEGREE SLOPES! Although I'd written 'Post Stroke on the entry form, there was no one around if I collapsed in the bush where brown snakes or dugites lurked. That thought kept me sharp, I tell you! No thanks! Actually, fear of falling probably got me through that last stage of the race!

I also had visions of a melodramatic ending, with people cheering and clapping, cameras flashing, handshakes, congratulations, all the hail-fellow-back-slapping-well-done-Petes! It had been years in the making, this crusade of mine! As we came round the last corner I was eager to see if any of my ridiculous images of a Rocky-type champion finish was waiting. "Yo Adrian, I did it!!!!"

I was so proud of myself! And why not? I'd proved to the world I was the first locked-in syndrome survivor to walked 12km in the history of the City to Surf, the first to complete the course so soon after ICU total quadriplegia - no stroke-busting drugs either! ALL MY OWN OBSESSIVE BEHAVOUR!

Yes, it's in capitals because I'd worked so bloody hard to get there. From the first millimetres in my thumb to pushing pillows in rehab to 12 incredible kilometres! Whoooowhoo!!

But nobody was there.

Scaffolding was still up, there was a lot of litter but, far from the ecstatic reception I'd anticipated, there was one girl on a golf buggy, a few tents and thousands of bottles of Powerade.

Although nothing could completely dampen my euphoria, I was deflated. It would have been nice for my feat to at least be witnessed by the organisers. Thank God for David who recorded the achievement for the medical world! The kind young girl on the buggy apologised that everyone had gone, handed out the Powerade and found a Finisher's medal which she presented to me. I felt honoured to have received it from such a worthy source, and the event was videoed for all my Facebook friends to see!

Of course, this wasn't the end of the story.

After the victory came the price; three days of pain and stiffness like I'd never felt in my life, not even in my army days, and toes so blistered and bloodied that my socks were welded on. Jade helped me remove them by soaking my feet beforehand, but I couldn't walk for ages, leaving me feeling quite sorry for myself.

Then I got the phone call. It was from a news company called 'Today Tonight' and somehow they'd heard about my City to Surf victory. Was I prepared to give an interview? Obviously I was keen to talk about my recovery - after all, I wanted people disabled by stroke and brain injury to take hope from my story. I also wanted to air my view on how the marathon should be safer for all participants, through electronic tagging, for instance. So I agreed to be interviewed – as long as they didn't make me sound like a whinging Pom! Little did I realise I was opening a can of worms!!*

Apparently, due to my late arrival, I'd held up the city of Perth with hours of road closures, virtually bringing the whole place to a halt - a noteworthy event in itself - which, when combined with the triumph and pathos of my story, proved hard to resist. So, from nobody seeing me arrive at the Finishing Line, suddenly we had a million viewers on prime-time TV! Not what I'd planned at all, but I honestly believe God wanted to help me reach the 'damned' out there that day, opening the path for other disabled survivors. The message went out – with rehabilitation, the power of the mind, and sheer stubbornness, it's amazing what can be achieved. I hope many others attempt the City to Surf – and it should be safer after my unplanned news clip, I'll bet!

Even so, I also got some cyber abuse, people saying exactly as I feared, "Go home, you whinging Pom", and a mix of hurtful comments from those who'd no idea what that walk took to accomplish.

In 2016 David Blacker, Peter Kilby (a teacher mate from Shents), a chemist named Martin and I smashed 16km. This was an event held by John Hughes, the biggest car dealer in Western Australia, whom I met when I received the Pride of Australia medal in 2013, an annual award organised by Perth Now. The medal was beautiful – it had stars on it like Captain America!

That first TV interview created quite a stir during what was possibly the biggest year of my struggle, leading to an increasing level of media interest. The 'Sunday Night' show, from a national TV network, flew all the way to Western Australia to interview me and Jade. I found it hard to believe someone was interested in us after treading such a lonely road of pain and obsession.[+]

We were asked to meet the camera crew in the Pan Pacific Hotel in the heart of Perth – all expenses paid, including taxi fares! Knowing how big this show was in Australia, we were extremely excited, a bit scared and smartly dressed for what was a very, very emotionally charged day for us both. This was the first time I'd told my story in public and I still find it hard to watch. Seeing Jade cry hurts to this day, and my own loss of self-control is really embarrassing.

My voice is very different now.

*City to Surf interview
https://www.youtube.com/watch?v=qzvIRrnc860

+The Sunday Night Show interview – Parts 1 and 2
https://petercoghlan.com/2014/01/17/peter-coghlan-stars-in-the-sunday-night-show-perth/

Chapter 36

We also featured in 'That's Life' magazine that year. I say 'that year', but to be honest, I've lost track of everything - things were just happening much too fast for me, and I wasn't sleeping. My head was in overdrive, dragging up all the old memories I hadn't yet dealt with and was trying to bury. What to say, how I came across to other survivors, just everything!

And, on top of everything else, I finally opened up to my GP (Dr Lucinda), who thought I was probably suffering with PTSD and so referred me to a psychologist, this was seven years after being in Shents.

It was all too much!

By now, I'd set up a website and it wasn't long before emails started arriving from around the world from stroke and brain injury survivors or their friends and relatives, asking for advice. Some of their stories broke my heart and, naturally, I wanted to help. In a way, it was healing for me too. It felt good to be of some use again. So, as soon as I could drive, I became a volunteer at Shenton Park, a role I took very seriously. I felt I needed to speak to the frightened survivors because I understood; I recognised their shock and pain and, sadly, knew all too well that the world into which they'd been tossed (so suddenly) held nothing and no one to inspire them.

Eventually, I found out why no doctors, nurses or therapists could answer that million-dollar question: "Will I be okay again?" The fact is, every case is different, making it impossible for even the most experienced consultant to predict a patient's recovery. Added to that, some people are highly litigious, taking medical staff to court over lots of incidents at the drop of a hat.

But then I realised that I could say something which the professionals couldn't! And I always spoke the truth.

Make no mistake, recovery from stroke or brain injury is hard work. Each stage of my recovery took months of effort – but to any survivor out there I can only say this, "Keep trying." It takes time and effort but, if you never give up and keep on trying, even when progress is slow, you'll continue to make gains, I'm sure! Remember, recovery is your job now and you CAN do it. Just keep trying and be determined, you'll surprise yourself!

Now that's a big thing to hear, but essential advice if you're as lost as I and those poor survivors in Shents were! I just wish I could have visited that helpless, hopeless me in ward G51, a thought that spurred me on and made me realise this was my path; to prove that, in many cases, the power of a determined brain was key to blowing the rule book away.

There's just one problem, my obsession to help and fuel survivors came at a big cost in my personal life. What I'm about to tell you is a something you may have seen coming – but I certainly didn't.

It has to do with Jade. With my short temper, tiredness, obsession to answer emails, exhaustion from hydro, volunteer work, walking and exercising, it was "Jade do this!" "Jade do that!" "Jade! Jade! Jade!" These incessant demands, along with the poverty that was killing us, eventually forced us apart and I began sleeping in the spare room due to my insomnia. It was total bollocks! The poor girl just couldn't take any more of me and my life.

At 7.30am, Jade left for work in her cheap, little white Hyundai and never came back; and quite frankly, who would blame her?

It was three years before we reconnected via messenger. Over the years Jade had had to deal with everything. The fact is, I refused to seek help - not a clever approach – and Jade didn't know what she'd done to deserve how I treated her, the way I shut her out. I just couldn't talk to anyone. Just couldn't.

And now I'd lost her. Almost every day, it was like I had a skip bin on my chest so that I could hardly breathe! I'd fall asleep and dream I could hear her car pull up outside, that she'd come in, kiss me and say, "I couldn't leave you, Stupid." Then I'd wake up, feeling sick with the sense of loss.

Crying, I'd get down on my knees, yelling to God: "Why is this life so f***in' shit? I don't deserve this! Why me…?" wailing in pain so loudly that the whole street must have heard!

"I'm being punished… but what have I done? Please God, tell me… Show me why… I hate my life!" I screamed into my pillow so hard I went dizzy. During those first weeks without Jade, I felt more lost than ever in my life. Just functioning was hard and I almost gave up. Almost …

This is where I have to thank my Mum from the bottom of my soul because, at the lowest day of my life, after I'd spent hours staring at the floor, she sent me a link that clicked a button in my brain and saved me from losing my sanity forever! It was Eminem's rap song: 'I'm Not Afraid!"

Thanks Eminem, you were the turning point in my world, the world I'd virtually given up on! Some of your songs were just words in my head, but you sure have a gift, bro! You can motivate millions.

The fuse in my head was lit. From the sorry, self-pitying state I was in, I suddenly became an atomic bomb, brimming with hope-fuelled energy!

"Right, Pete… You're not f***in' done yet! Nobody counts me out… I will be all I can be! I'm stronger than this. Get up and fight, God damn it!" And with those words, psychotic Pete was born!

For many years I never really knew me, if that makes sense. But from now on, I had a renewed sense of purpose. I was at the gym almost every day, waiting at the doors from 5.30am, and for the next 6 months I took to the water, warm water, as Cancer signs do in trouble, like I mentioned before.

To help pay my rent, I started a cleaning job through Create Employment, an agency that helps disabled people get back to work – and, guess what? More bleeding toilets, only in a cake factory this time; seemed quite fitting really! I felt like shit and my life was being constantly flushed away!

Looking back, I honestly don't know how I stuck that bloody cake factory. It took everything I had to get there, clock in and grab my mop bucket without slipping on the slimy, cake mix floor. Even the mop bucket seemed to be against me, as I had to put one foot on it to keep it steady while I squeezed out the mop. Simple enough you'd think? Wrong! Trying to balance on one leg while lifting the other was insanely difficult, and I tried to grasp the wall to steady myself with an arm so weak it was just a f***in' joke! Quite frankly, I hated that job. Apart from the physical problems, I got shit from young staff who thought they knew everything and criticised my every move. "Oh, it's okay for some, ey! Have a break whenever you want!" yelled one cocky young lad. I was eating a banana for energy! Had he said that to the former me, he'd have been smacked in the throat!

I was pissed. Really pissed!! I hated that job!

Chapter 37

Protein powder, bananas, disgusting concoctions with capsicums, banana, cocoa, porridge and chia seeds - anything remotely healthy. Eating raw broccoli in my car... I was completely crazed at the time. A suitable case for a straight-jacket, I'd say!

My lonely nights after the gym were a bit like reruns of Rocky Balboa doing squats and stretches on the floor; best I could do was standing and holding my arms out at the side of me for as long as possible, shoulders burning so bad but just about bearable, knowing this burn was gonna help me win, something I'd learned from previous karate. I could hear my Sensei willing me on: "Hold it... hold it... hold it... okay, relax and breathe ... Again!"

At times, I was so mad I was a danger to myself. I mean, I'd forget that I was still quite vulnerable. For example, one month or so after Jade left me, around Christmas, I was stupid enough to drive to the local shops – assuming there'd be free disabled bays! Idiot!

Seeing a couple of seniors coming back to their car, I pulled over in the car park with my hazard lights flashing clearly! (Remember, I was a lit fuse at any given time!) This lady, (ha, can't say that she acted like one) pulled alongside and said, "You don't own the f***in' car park, you know!" Well, that atomic bomb detonated.

I reached for my disabled pass and stuck it in her face, shaking badly and said: "I'm bloody disabled!"

"P*** off!" came the ladylike reply. "

"You get my f***in' shopping then" I said!

I could hardly stop shaking! As a result of a stroke, clonus involuntary muscular contractions (uncontrollable shaking) can happen, which makes you even madder. Then you can just burst out crying! As for me, I started hitting the steering wheel, screaming my head off! And with that performance, my tormenter drove away, probably thinking "he needs help!"

I DID need help... help from the system I suppose! But I was too proud to lose myself on paper! I certainly didn't want this at the end of my CV - "Dangerous lunatic post-stroke."

I had visions of Sarah Connor, from Terminator 2, doing chin-ups in a padded room! Hard to forget that I was restrained with blue rubber foam pads in hospital! I was scared of myself, but more scared of what would happen if sat down and let someone get inside my head.

As for my job, one more reason I hated it so much was they tried to get me charged with harassment! Yes, bloody harassment!!!

I attempted to get on with all the staff, yet had never previously worked with females - just builders and squaddies. So at the factory, I tried to be as pleasant as I could and stay out of trouble. Unfortunately, I made the mistake of complimenting one of the female staff on her shoes, or perfume, can't remember which, but I certainly didn't get personal or over-familiar.

Then one day I was cleaning a sodding toilet and had a phone call from my personal trainer Cheri from the gym. She had some amazing news.

"Pete, I just wanted to tell you someone has donated 10 training sessions worth $350 to help you with your recovery!"

Well, I just was so gob-smacked and touched, I cried, broke down right there and then, in the proximity of this staff member! She came up to me with another lady and asked if I was okay.

I felt really stupid and tried to stop crying and control myself, but couldn't. That's when I made a mistake I will never make in my life again - I touched her shoulders with my wrists for a second then buried my tears in my one good arm. Not everyone reading this will understand, but you know when you reach out in pain.

Now, I was also at fault by ending an email months earlier saying, "Have a great weekend mate x". It was the 'x' that did it!

Shit, I learned a lot that year, that feeling of being accused of harassment was so hurtful to me, and so far from my nature. Harassment just wasn't me! But then, I shouldn't really have been working at that stage of recovery! Had I seen a councillor or sought support from Centrelink they would have said that I had too much to deal with. But I didn't want to let anybody see I was weak! Of course, it's not weak to get help, but I was too angry and dealing with so much loss...

Yes, with stroke you lose everything - your confidence, your personality, your identity.

I was a big-ass bag of pain and grief and my only salvation was Kingsway Gym! I practically lived there, trying not to let the personal trainers see my tears on the squat press, my favourite machine. When on the bike, I started to look around at people working out on machines I could only dream of using. But gradually, month by month, I advanced to new, more challenging machines because I was so hungry.

In hindsight, the anger Jade had left me with was literally a gift tailor made for the new Pete. One night, about a month before Jade left, I prayed for the motivation to keep going, little did I know my prayers would be answered. Four years later, I can see it so clearly! The powers that be were not punishing me; they were answering my prayers, even though I didn't believe in all that stuff! Only the Force could know what would drive me the hardest.

That explains why I waited to complete my story. Back then, I couldn't have written one positive word and the Old Bill would have been dragging me off to a hospital psychiatric ward.

And, months later, I was again taken aback by events! This you will not believe, but I swear on my life and anyone I ever cared for, that it's true!

I rented a small apartment from my mate Brian (Brain I call him, due to my bad spelling), but was struggling to afford it, so moved into my old marital home which we'd left to go to Thailand and was now owned by Dave. Bad move! I stayed in one of the bedrooms I tiled and painted before my stroke, and every inch of my former home caused memories to flood into my mind. I couldn't even shower because of flashbacks to that nightmare hospital night. And my bedroom was so small I was sleeping with my weights on top of the bed.

I cracked again, crying on my bed and begging someone to hear my prayers. I actually called to God, like you do when you're desperate no matter what your beliefs or lack of them. You just do...

"God, please, please! I just can't operate like this... I can't be here... Please I need your help... Get me out of here... PLEASE!" I was pathetic, desperate, just about finished. Life had punched and punched and punched me again. I wanted out.

That week, breaking into my introverted lost world of auto pilot, I had a phone call. It was an old mate from my 457 visa days. "Mike! Good to hear your voice, bro!"

He was telling me about his wife Jeanette, how she was on dialysis for her kidneys - or was it liver - I forget now? He invited me round for a yarn and cuppa! Quite honestly, I wasn't really in the mood to for conversation yet I believe my visit was actually a sign. Another prayer heard.

Whether you're a believer or not, this freaked me out.

After a rather brave story about Jeanette's new life - also against the odds, Mike says, "I've got something to show you, Pete. Come with me." We walked past Nelson, the Aussie Blue Heeler dog, to the side of the house where Mike pointed to a tin garage conversion basically, say 4mx10m from memory! It wasn't plastered and had no coving, so you could see through to where the wall and ceiling met.

"You can have it for $150 a week all in - including Internet! Do you want it?"

No curtains or flooring, but I could operate here! Space for my bed, desk, weights, toilet and shower, even space for a microwave on my desk with a kettle! Perfect for a guy on his uppers, albeit a tin garage!

"Yes Mike, awesome bro!!! I want it..! When can I move in?"

"Tomorrow if you want, I have a twin-axle trailer to help with your stuff." I shook his hand with joy in my soul, thankful to escape the memories that plagued my every second in Marangaroo. Someone had heard my prayer!

Returning to my car, I stopped in my tracks. There was a 3ft wooden cross in their garden saying, "JESUS LIVES HERE." No words...

Who am I to question what the Force is? I just know I felt like a Jedi Knight again - the Force was with me!

Chapter 38

I was in there like a rat up a drainpipe! It was a savage day but nothing was stopping me getting away from the stroke zone of broken memories. The rain was ridiculous; when it rains in Australia it can be almost a year's rain in a weekend!

In my positive way, I turned it around in my head, told myself it had to be a blessing to wash the tears and pain out of my life. "Today my life changes," I vowed!

All my things were saturated - although I only had a few clothes and a bed. My barbell weights were wet too – oh, and my 3 medals - namely Army Service, Best Rifle Shot Recruit, and my Pride of Australia Medal which I slept with under my pillow - I couldn't let it out of my sight!

I also had a gold chain, the one I wore when I hobbled out of Shenton Park hospital, but I was so skint after Jade left that I had to pawn it. 7oz of handmade gold specially made for me by a young apprentice, who put my initials (PC) on the clasp.

Although funds were low, I had enough for a few weeks rent and my sister was struggling too, so I put $500 in an envelope with a card saying "thanks for saving my life!"

Being able to help my sister out was such a special thing for me. After the stroke, $500 to me was massive, but I didn't care. Giving is the most amazing thing, I've come to realise - a greater blessing for the giver than for the receiver. And when you can't move or do anything for others it's even more special, magical even.

Now I was flat broke again, but I had my tin shed with Internet! Mick and Jeanette left me to myself in my tin castle and I was grateful for that; I needed that time on my own. It had really started to sink in that I'd have to continue my battle alone and I felt totally lost. My passenger seat felt weird, as it would, I guess, for anyone who loses a companion, a person who's sat next to them for over a decade. A strange sensation that's hard to explain – almost as though the silhouette's still there, yet the substance has gone.

I was going to prove I was worth not giving up on, so help me God! No one was going to stop me! Looking back, I honestly believe my grief at Jade's leaving was the most amazing gift, tailor-made fuel to get me through the next two years; pain with the power to heal, pain that triggered a switch as no drug on the market could have done. I was virtually pulling the doors off the gym!

For so long, life just seemed to be cleaning toilets, gym, long walks, protein powders, healthy food, warm water movements and my volunteer job at Fiona Stanley Hospital; which was a brand new, state-of-the-art 'space station', reminiscent of Star Wars! Robots delivering meals, a futuristic layout, computers and TVs for patients – it's unbelievable! Welcome to 2015!

The Volunteer Task Force (VTF) was a great healer for my mental and emotional wounds, helping me focus on positives when I was so angry at life and at being abandoned, which I certainly didn't view as a blessing at the time. But how could I be angry when talking to frightened stroke patients, pushing their wheelchairs to the café, or just sitting by their beds. This was no chore for me, as I got as much back from them as they gained from me. Life after a stroke or head injury can be very worrying; no, that's an understatement, terrifying comes closer, haunted by the seemingly unanswerable question: "Will I ever be the same?"

Yes, that job saved me, gave me a lot, reminded me that even in my tin shed I was doing well, that, instead of dwelling on what was lost, I should be thankful for what I'd managed to claw back. Another, big plus, I got to see my nurses and therapists, which made me so proud. Walking into Ward A – MY Ward – and sanitising my hands made me quite nostalgic. I came to love the familiar scent of the foam gel cleanser, it was like my fix; having smelled it on everyone who came near me for so long, it was like a home smell, comforting. How mad is that?

Speaking of home, after moving into my penthouse, I soon realised I was not alone. Along with the occasional cricket jumping on my face at night, the rain also washed a few spiders in through the cracks between the walls and ceiling, which were still un-plastered with no cornice. Not that I'm inhospitable or anything; I just wasn't best pleased if a spider crawled over my sheets!

Much of my time was spent posting strong, positive quotes on Facebook: "I'm ok, I'm tough blah blah blah..." when truth was I'd actually lost a bit of my soul and needed to pull myself out of my lonely, desperate situation!

ADAPT! IMPROVISE! OVERCOME! My old Cheshire regiment had drilled this mantra into us and it now resounded as never before. "No!" I told myself, "25058396 PTE Coghlan's story does NOT end in this tin garage!" (Grateful as I was to have a roof!)

As I listened to the rain and thunder I lay awake just trying to see a future! Here I was, alone, living on handouts from Centrelink. I had no direction, I'd been kicked to the kerb by life and I knew if I didn't soon make changes, I'd be flushed away by the cake factory toilets!

On my next volunteer day, I asked my speechy David for some career advice. "David, I've no idea what to do anymore. I'm lost. I come to hospital all the time because it's the only positive place for me, the only place I feel of any use!" Part of me felt safe there too; another fallout from stroke is a constant fear that your brain's going wrong somehow. It's terrifying.

David thought for a moment. "Have you considered an Allied Health Assistant course?"

"What's that?"

"Well, not everyone in physio or occupational therapy departments are therapists, you know! Most of them work under the therapist as Allied Health Assistants."

David had just turned on a light bulb! "Wow! You mean I could work alongside my heroes?"

"Yes, Pete!" David chuckled. And with that thought, I walked off Ward A with a dream and a direction...

Chapter 39

I was bloody sick of cleaning and getting the shits from the odd staff, that bloody cake factory dished me up some shit! I was fed up to the back teeth!

Thank goodness for my barber D-Pac who let me share my frustrations with him. Most barbers are natural born listeners – or maybe they just learn to nod and pretend they care while customers unload their crap; they should be called therapists! Not D-Pac, he wasn't like that. After my rant, he said: "Pete what you need is to work for yourself."

"Ha-ha, like what, mate? I'm weak as piss!"

"Well, you can walk and talk now. Why not set up a gardening round?"

"No, money mate! That ain't going to happen. But great advice, I'll take it on board D-Pac."

As he finished my (almost) buzz haircut, he suggested we go for a coffee. "I want to do you a favour, Pete! Not because I feel sorry for you but because I know you deserve a chance after struggling so long." He was well aware of my break up and living arrangements.

"I have a roller, a lawn mower, an edging grinder and a whipper snipper (that's a strimmer to you and me!) Do you think you could run a lawn maintenance round?" I doubted it.

"Not sure I could push a roller mate, not with my arms!"

But D-Pac was undeterred. "No Pete, it's powered simply; just *stop*, *go*, *break* and *accelerator*. Come and take a look, it's in my garage."

"Wow really?!"

"It's no cheap mower, Pete. It's a good bit of kit!"

"Wow D-Pac, I don't know what to say." The usual 'thank you' seemed totally inadequate, but I said it anyway and jumped at the chance. D-Pac was not in it for gain. By this time, I'd known him for a year or two, a 'salt of the Earth' gentleman if ever there was. Yes, there are a few left - found that out on my road! You think the world's all bad, but sometimes, when you're in need, people do surprise you! And, if you're reading this, D-Pac, you'll always be a legend! Thank you, thank you and thank you! That job was the answer to my prayers!

No more slippery cake floors, whinging teens, toilets, or harassment charges (I wasn't convicted) but came very close.

For almost a year, I cut lawns, proudly towing a trailer behind my commodore and, come to think of it, with all that walking it was an ideal, tailor-made rehab job for Pete. The cash was useful too, of course! Although it wasn't much, as I wasn't quick enough to clean up, mentally and physically it helped to mend a very broken man. I didn't find my sudden abandonment easy to accept at the time, but I understand now.

Now, being a Registered Sole Trader, 'Pete Coghlan Services', gave me back some pride - not that I was above cleaning, which I still did at weekends. It was just that NOW I could think and work without any crap!

Time to reflect is so important; I'd always worked while sorting my problems out, something most blokes need. That's why I support a new club over here called 'Men's Shed'. We're not like the fairer sex; we don't have girls' groups with wine and hugs. I don't mean to be stereo-typing anyone, it's just that women connect a bit differently, whereas blokes don't always need to talk about their feelings; it's more a case of work and then maybe open up to a workmate a bit at a time, while processing issues! I think that goes for most blokes, well, certainly for me. Instead of seeing a shrink, telling this story has been my way of dealing with things! And hopefully it will resonate with others in a similar position.

The *Men's Shed* seems to be working well here in Perth. I wish it was global, because I met guys with really bad shit happening to them, some of it truly heart breaking; one guy lost his entire family in a car fire – all his kids!

Yes, *Men's Sheds* are a "must" these days. They're just that too, a big shed where some of them (the *Men's Sheds*) do woodwork, others metal work. They are places for all men who pride themselves in mateship; looking out for each other, checking up on each other, noticing if someone doesn't show, helping to get each other through bad times. Bit by bit.

Over the next year, my grass cutting job began to get hard. It wasn't an easy job anyway, as it involved a lot of walking, but the great Aussie summer really broke me with its flies! Wafting the beggars away was probably my best arm rehab; Australian bush flies have to be the most irritating, most persistent little shits on this planet! Up ya nose, in ya eyes, on ya lips... arrrrgggggghhhhh! Mowing wasn't quite as bad as my previous jobs, though; as a bricklayer you never have a hand free! Try wafting flies with a bloody brick or a trowel full of mortar!

The discomfort wasn't my real motive for quitting, however. I just needed to help people, an urge that burned inside me. So, I serviced D-Pac's gear and gave it back to him – and, you know what? He gave me $50 for servicing everything and thanked me! He thanked ME! Unbelievable!

My circle these days is pure titanium. Like I said earlier, it's only through tough times real friends are forged!

Chapter 40

On leaving Ward A at Fiona Stanley Hospital, I met a Scottish lass I knew called Michelle – an Occupational Therapist, or so I thought! But now I knew different.

"So, you're an Allied Health Assistant, ey!" I said. Michelle gazed back at me, slightly bemused.

"Yeah Pete. Why?"

"Because... I'M going to be one, mate! Whooooohooooo!"

"Really Pete?" Michelle was more excited than me! "I think you'd be awesome, especially after your experience! Go for it Pete! Yaaay!"

Her enthusiasm was encouraging, giving me belief in my direction! That afternoon, David (my Speech Pathologist) helped too, sending me useful links about the course and outlining what was involved: recognising healthy body systems; recognising behaviours; everything from infection control to policies and procedures! I was in like a snake down a rabbit hole!

"Yes, Hi ... My name's Peter Coghlan. I'm calling to enrol in this year's Allied Health Assistant Cert III course, please."

Pens, folders, new bag (well from the salvos, a place I frequently visited!) Centrelink loaned me enough money for the course and I also qualified for a concession! It was on! At the age of 38, I was officially a student, limping into lectures. No ex-locked-in patient had ever attempted such a course and, even though I could now walk and talk, they weren't ready for me. But, determined to follow my heroes into action, I was ready for them! My goal was simple: To help others get through a day.

Once the semester was underway, I began to see that, with one or two lecturers, some of the lessons being taught were not actually applied. For example, disability considerations for one! The help I'd requested just wasn't available; the mouse was on the wrong side (opposite my good hand) so I couldn't use it, and our class was constantly moving up and down stairs. Although I could manage stairs by then, we always seemed to get moved after I set up for the lesson! It wasn't funny. One particular lecturer would insist on moving to another classroom every bloody time I got my books out! Part of the problem was my punctuality; I was always early, set up ready to go, twiddling a pen. Not that I expected special treatment, mind – just a little consideration for my disability. I soon realised, however, that a lot of teachers are just that – teachers. Great at passing on knowledge but not always empathetic to life's experience and distinctly lacking in bedside manner!

I have to say it really got me down that first semester. To add to my woes, there was no parking at TAFE, so I had to keep moving my car. Imagine me hobbling back to my car three times a day, then trying to catch up with my notes; when just a few months previously I could hardly hold a pen. On the plus side, I managed to keep up (just) thanks to mum, who helped me with assignments or presentations on how body systems work. I have forgotten a lot, but somehow things stuck in my head. Much as I disliked her teaching style, one of my lecturers taught me something extremely vital:

DR MIC URINE!

This memory aid has helped me remember 10 body systems - (there are actually 11, but nailing 10 is quite an achievement, I feel):

*Digestive system
*Respiratory system
*Musculoskeletal system
*Immune system
*Cardiovascular system
*Urinary system
*Reproductive system
*Integumentary system
*Nervous system
*Endocrine system

I think Lymphatic is the 11[th,] but can't swear to it! At any rate this is a pretty good way to remember these systems, which I'd repeat to myself whilst munching my Kellogg's and writing them down for good measure. Yep, there's nothing like a good dose of Dr Mic Urine for breakfast!

Oh, I was keen alright, yet I started lagging behind when Safety in the Workplace units were introduced. I felt I was a problem. In reality, I wasn't... just that I started to believe all the negatives or obstacles that were put to me – usually flagged by the word 'unfortunately'.

"Unfortunately, Pete, you'll always be considered a potential risk in the workplace, but that's not to say you ARE – just that employers will probably think twice after learning your story!" These words pretty nearly destroyed me!

Possibly, the lecturer thought about what he'd said that night because the next day he approached. "Pete, about our conversation yesterday... I think it came out the wrong way. What I meant to say was... well, I just wanted you to know everyone's a risk in the workplace... that's all I was saying, really."

I knew he was probably covering tracks; despite my problems, I wasn't wet behind the ears, but he was a good bloke so I knew he was behind me, even though his first comment still knocked my confidence. But I was gonna do this! Believing I had a better understanding than anyone on that course, I was not giving up!

Another bugbear during the course was the interminable 'Death by Powerpoint'. Slide after slide for hours every day! God! I hated it and not much stayed in my head, either! I was a people person, that's what this course was about - I wanted to be with people. At this stage, I was already 500 hours strong in volunteer work; I had a good bedside manner and I knew how to be with people. That part came so naturally to me. I wasn't feeling the course!

In my view, the course wasn't meant for people who'd been through the system. It was for clever, fast-learning students and to stop the wrong people slipping through the net (I guess), to make sure they could speak English and had basic hygiene skills, providing a fairly basic entry level to the health system.

Not that it was easy! I use the word 'basic' advisedly, as it was far from basic to me. It felt like the government said "Okay, we need this, this, this, this and this, oh and this, this and this! And we'll cram all these elements into one semester and charge a few grand per student!"

It was a bit full on for me, but after the stroke and 25 years out of a classroom it's gonna be, ey! Case in point: The best allied health assistants in Shenton Park, the ones who got me through those dark days, were not qualified on paper; in those days, my course simply didn't exist. I'm not saying a qualification is a bad thing; it's just that I came from an apprenticeship and, to me, there's nothing better than solid hands-on experience which draws the real person out. As an apprentice, school leavers find out if they like the job before committing time and money, while employers can see first-hand if their staff and clients work well together.

Anyway, I'm just lucky enough to see both sides I guess. I don't like to speak negatively.

As for the course, I passed more than half the units before having to pull out, purely because I couldn't deal with everything that was happening at the time! Firstly, some dumb-arse wrote off my modified commodore!

I'd driven to the city to visit Lee, a 21-year old stroke survivor I'd met through my volunteer job. As her left side had been severely damaged, Lee was granted government housing - something offered to me which, over three bloody years, never materialised. I wasn't bitter at all, but the system is pretty messed up.

After taking Lee to the local shops for a squeezy bottle of honey (she couldn't open jars) along with special funnels to transfer the honey across, we had some lunch together and I set off home.

Waiting for some traffic lights to turn green near a John Hughes car lot, I gazed covetously at all the beautiful new motors and, with just 15 dollars in my pocket, wondered how anyone could afford a brand new car, $30,000? And then it happened! A car came through the junction on red...... Oh.. my.. God!

The car T-boned the rear left side and began to spin. It had left the ground and was spinning towards me! I couldn't reverse; I was trapped, locked-in, so to speak! I pulled a stupid face and braced for the impact!

BANG! It landed right on my bonnet! Just like that! My car was a gonna! Glass everywhere but, thank God, no injuries. Shaking and stunned but blessedly intact! I got out, I rang the RAC, and left the madness of the scene like a character in a Jason Bourne movie, only not as cool – Matt makes even a bloody limp look awesome! In the big truck taking me home I just stared out of the window, unable to believe how things had turned against me. I was past the angry stage, not feeling much at all, just numb, staring aimlessly.

For three sodding weeks I had to get six buses to college every day! Three there and three back! Leaving my tin room at 6am to catch three buses was a privilege, I knew that, but I was so tired of living from hurdle to hurdle and feeling very much alone. I was just a machine going through the motions. Three buses, death by PowerPoint, changing classrooms, three buses home, gym, homework, then drop... and, to make life *really* exciting, with bouts of insomnia thrown in. Months of this made me quit! Yes, I quit something; it really damaged my pride!

A few weeks before I left the course, I had yet another disaster I'll never forget. As I set off for home, the temperature hit 38^0C; not nice after a stressed day in the library where I'd been trying to use a PC, a complex procedure for a guy who'd only used a laptop or phone.

The bus had air conditioning although there wasn't much point, as the doors kept opening all the time, and I yearned to get home and shower, desperate to escape the suffocating heat. But the bus had other ideas... 'Shit its last gas', didn't it! Broke down! I groaned inwardly. "Ohhh no! Not today!" The car last week and bus this week! "Argggghhhhhh!"

A couple of mothers in front of me were... erm... a little lacking in parental skills, shall we say! Yeah, well, let's go with that; which in no way describes the torrent of abuse they rained down upon their offspring! I'm just saying the truth when I say that it actually made me see why some kids don't stand a chance in life!

"Oy! stop ya f-in' crying 'n' stay in that f-in' seat, or... I'll f-in' stab you with that f-in' pen!" Loud too! You could have cut the air with a knife, yet nobody on the bus said a damn word. I was no better, just gazing out the window, feeling so sorry for those children and, if possible, even more depressed than ever. I just wanted to stop all the madness; to pull back, re-group, get more sleep and maybe assess the damage! My only 'happy place' at the time was the pool, where I could slide, crablike, into the water.

My Dad came to Perth about that time, saw where I was living, sat on my bed and sighed, "I feel like crying!"

"Dad, it's all I can afford and Mick and Jeanette are brilliant." This was an understatement, as they looked after me so well, bringing me home-made soup and inviting me for the odd meal. Not many landlords do that! But Dad couldn't be consoled.

"No wonder you're sinking! You've no car, no kitchen, no money - why haven't you got that 1-bedroom apartment yet? You were approved!"

"I ring them, Dad... they just keep telling me there's a waiting list." And what a list! Many people on it were in a far worse state than me. Priority went to victims of domestic violence (understandably), followed by asylum seekers; some of the stories I've heard are just awful -

families hacked up in their village by meat cleavers! Bloody sick! The World's sick!

"Everyone needs help, Dad!"

"But what about YOU? You still qualify. You just can't live in a garage, son!" He paused and rubbed his eyes, trying to take stock of my situation.

"Well, now I've seen what you're up against, I'll do my best to help you." Good old Dad, always there in a crisis! In that moment, I felt like a kid again, looking up to my Dad, trusting him to make everything right!

Another great support was David Blacker, my neurologist, who'd written to the housing department on my behalf. In his opinion, "Peter needs somewhere to get some grounding after locked-in syndrome," adding that my prospects of getting back to work were promising. Sadly, his letter didn't make a difference to the struggling housing system, but I was well aware how lucky people in the western world actually are. Had I lived in many other countries, I'd probably be eating what crawled over me at night! I've always tried to see the glass that way... half full. Well, you've got to, ey! Still, there were times I felt deflated; it seemed I'd come to the land of milk and honey only to find bread and water. There were times I felt like crying. But it was not going to bash me down! I vowed, "I will make it!"

The gym held things together for me; I needed two things in my life - gym and hospital. When I wasn't pumping weights or cardio workouts at one location, I'd be helping stroke survivors at the other. I was back in my bubble.

Chapter 41

My self-worth was rapidly diminishing - not that I had much to start with, and jacking in my course didn't help much, so when this popped into my Inbox a few days later, I felt like someone was throwing me a bone. "Dear Peter, we have followed your progress from Shenton Park Rehabilitation and would like to invite you to this year's Harry Perkins Institute of Research symposium on...."

Well I was absolutely stunned! Un-be-liev-able. Oh-my-God! ME...in front of doctors, professors, neurologists - all the big guns, what the...? The invitation dragged me right out the depression wedge I was in, thank God too; I was so tired, mentally mostly, feeling a failure for quitting my course. I hated to fail; I had no direction again, you see. In this world, you have to have a goal or you go insane. Some people choose drink or drugs, but I needed positive things now.

That email saved me! Just having somebody recognise how hard I'd been trying, for year upon year. Up to that point, I felt forgotten by everyone; friends never once came to see me in my garage, only my mum, making this the loneliest period of my life.

Having just given birth to her second child, my sister Vicky was going through a low point too (postnatal depression) trying to survive each day, and frequently teary. I'm not sure children are something I ever wanted really, but Vicky and Brad's – a boy and a girl - are a joy to have around!

Months after my first speaking assignment, I was asked (by Head Lecturer, Zona) to talk to occupational therapy students at Curtin University, then to nurses at Sir Charles Gairdner and Armadale Hospital! I was so chuffed that someone wanted to meet me and hear my story. Such a difference to the world I left behind, a world full of people drinking, me doing my blokey bit at my bar, knocking on for a smoke and a chinwag. Then, having battled my way home from locked-in syndrome, everyone was chatting on Facebook, but few came to see me face to face. Despite wanting human interaction, I just seemed more disconnected than before! Friends would type: "Oh, we must catch up sometime" yet that 'sometime' never came. This was the same shit for years, so I started to make new friends, new circles, including my own circle of disabled friends to whom I could relate. Like Bryce.

Bryce was living with my mate Craig from Shenton Park and was a right character; he had the funniest attitude and a tragic story to tell, which he's given me permission to share. He's my age and at 18 was hit by a drunk driver; didn't stand a chance. The pissed-up bloke hit him with the bull-bars of his Ute, putting him in a coma. It took years for him to talk again. 22 years later, he still has speech issues; now not so much from impaired breath support, as he's not walking. Yet he's verbal enough to constantly abuse me, the git! Ha ha.

I would rather spend an evening checking on Bryce and getting pizzas in than prop up the bar like I used to. Having friends like Bryce puts my priorities in order, something other people just don't see until they're alone and broken themselves!

Alicia, a trainee nurse I met on the campus, got me a volunteer role in an aged care facility fairly close to my tin penthouse. That was an interesting few months indeed! If I told you I was on the knitting girl's team would you see me in a different light? Haha. Well I was. The little ladies just loved me, and they wanted me to sit and talk with them, so I did! They were awesome!

"Have you ever done crochet, Peter?" I had to admit to a distinct lack of skill in this area.

"You hold one needle like this, then like that... Get the thread with the crochet hook round the needle and pull through here."

The process had some kind of rhyme to it as well, like 'round the houses, pull it through'... I forget now! But I loved it because it was OT. My fine motor skills needed these ladies, to whom I was a real golden girl - and there was no one there to rip the crap out of me for being one either! LOL!

The dementia ladies liked me too, especially when I asked, "May I have this dance madam?" Then they'd smile like they were 18 again! I couldn't dance obviously, but here was my chance to try! I WAS DOING WHATEVER IT TOOK! Ok lads! I can see my mates ribbing me about this for years!

How much I hated dancing was no longer an issue. Slow dancing was a great way to start and now I view this experience as a privilege. Not that I leap onto the dance floor now, but at least I'll try if asked, whereas before I'd shy away and flatly refuse. Yes, the delicate frail old ladies were putting me through my paces all right and, because they wouldn't remember me the next week, when I asked them for a dance again as close to Prince Charming as I could, the same flattered look in their eyes every time. It was really special! A look I never got from girls before!

There was an ex-army bloke in the home who never socialised with anyone much - very tall, ramrod straight and very much a sergeant-major type! Not knowing how introverted he was, I just sat down and began talking, opening with an army tale about a great grouping at the ranges one day at 1000 metres. Well, that was it! The floodgates opened as he told me about his platoon and where they were based, his eyes misty at the memories. I found his old unit on Google with pictures of him and his mates, which really touched him, I know it did. And that was the moment. That was when I realised I could reach people, help them get through the day just as others had done for me. That was the moment I knew I could finish my bloody course! So I applied again, signing up for the following year at Joondalup Health Campus!

As for the old sergeant, I took him out for walks while I was there, something he'd never done 'in years', so I was told. It was hard to see so many residents staring into the distance with no fixed direction; just staring for ages as though they were looking back at life. I knew that look, I felt the pain they were experiencing; loss, mainly.

I also learned about boundaries when the sergeant, who'd obviously taken a shine to me, squeezed my left buttock! Never saw that coming, but I believe I handled it well by notifying the Allied Health Team who quickly put an action plan in place. No more walks down the lane, I'll tell ya that for nothing!

Chapter 42

"Give and you shall receive" - that's the saying, ey. I didn't fully understand that until I started to put it into practice. The 400+ hours I'd put in those 3-5 years had really taught me so much, giving me back far more than I put in for sure!

As well as giving me experience in dementia, my work at the home also increased my dexterity and helped me gain much needed confidence and self-worth. And when I started my allied health course the second year, I had a readymade placement for practical assessments, as the hospital gave me experience in my interpersonal skills too. Empathy came naturally to me, it seemed. So you see, if you make the effort yourself, nothing is a waste of time; it will all come into play at some point!

A few months before college started I saw an advertisement for a 16km John Hughes walk or 21km run around the Swan river. "Hmm, it's been two years since my 12km marathon," I mused to myself. "Should I? Could I?" The thought plagued me all day, so I rang David Blacker again.

"Hey, Dr Blacker... you fancy a 16km walk next weekend? You know... a little stroll by the river on a Sunday?" Ha-ha! Most people would have said, "Bugger off, Pete it's Sunday!" but not David, nor my mate Peter Kilby. Like brothers in arms, we were a force of positivity! Thanks lads, it meant a lot.

You need to keep challenging yourself and surrounding yourself with friends who will really put themselves out to help you achieve, people who'll just be there. That's such a wonderful gift in life, which I see so clearly now. It's not about what we have, the best things in life are indeed free; real friends. By challenging yourself, you'll always find them, I think.

We had a great day for our walk. There was no wind so the reflection of the city was almost a mirror in the Swan River, which looked stunning. Peter K got some great pictures, including one of me and David overlooking the river with the city behind it! I've used this picture on my Instagram and also my Twitter page. Actually, I believe I set a world record for a locked-in syndrome survivor, 16km with his own neurologist is pretty special, I reckon, a picture that marks history in the city of Perth. As for the John Hughes event, I don't think John even knew of my record. On the last few kilometres, my knee felt sore and I prayed it wasn't on the way out! I'd been pushing off that knee for years now, from my wheelchair, sofa, off the ground and, more recently, with the leg press to strengthen my weak side, trying to balance the power evenly.

Another blessing: My Health Assistant course at Joondalup was very different to the one we followed the previous year. The new TAFE campus was state-of-the-art with great parking facilities and the lecturers were heaven sent, I swear it! All thanks to Jenny Campbell, Kelly Milner and David Pelusey. Wow, what a team! More than just lecturers, they'd worked as therapists for years and, through practical experience, had developed that special bedside manner – a quality you either have or you don't, a fact I felt infinitely qualified to know.

They realised that my issues in learning, were not in retaining information, but in sheer concentration. Being half deaf in one ear, I found it hard to concentrate with all the background noise in class, while the stupid riddle scenarios we'd been given the term before just didn't make sense, not even when the teachers sat down with me on my own and read each scenario out to me! Personally, I don't see the point in trying to catch you out with scenarios; it's not a good learning style for me, I guess. I had more experience than most, having not only lived through it but also due to my volunteer work. Scenarios may work on someone freshly entering the health system, but I wasn't a reader. I'd read a few pages and then think, "Who was Frank?" several pages later! I was never a scholar!

That being said, after all this writing, I will actually start *reading* now. Now I know I can do, it as long as I have complete silence. Come to think of it, that must be why I failed at school – classrooms are definitely not for me, and if it wasn't for my awesome lecturers I'd have failed a second time, for sure. I've highlighted this point because I feel the world we now live in is all paperwork and fails to see the person behind it. I saw a few great natural carers fail that course, failed by having too much placed in front of them in a mere 6 months. Some had small children... No way could I have done it with kids!

Anyway, after qualifying, I got the chance to highlight all my pros and cons at the university's TEDAN Professional Personal Development day to which I'd been invited as a guest speaker, a great boost after feeling so pathetic!

Glad I tried again. Thanks to my very special lecturers, I made history, becoming (I can definitely confirm) the first man to qualify for Allied Health Assistance, Certificate III after recovering from locked-in syndrome, an achievement recorded in Training Matters magazine for TAFE. How can I be so sure? Well, it was a new course at the time, but maybe another ex-locked-in survivor will apply before long.

There was one hiccup! I had to be passed off on a few more practical assessments that couldn't be done at my volunteer home for the aged. Thank God for Michelle, the CEO of a non-profit organisation in Perth.

Chapter 43

The Mayor of Wanneroo, Tracey Roberts, had taken me under her wing, as she had done for so many in her city, and introduced me to support work through a friend of hers called Helen. It was Helen who got me the interview that set me off on my first real job in health care.

I limped into the interview all-smart and sat on the sofa to wait for my turn, not super confident but feeling I had something worthwhile to offer. Problem was, I could overhear the interview taking place before mine. Well, I was sinking by the second! This Canadian girl was rattling off her experience - working with Autism, Down syndrome, behaviours of concern, the kids in different countries whom she'd cared for... and I glanced at my own CV - military, building, and driving qualifications! But, I did have experience in volunteer work! Thank God I put myself out! And I had my story – 'lived experience' they call it. When my turn came, I was totally honest, explaining everything as clearly as I could and, halfway through my Certificate III Allied Health Assistance course saga, the panel looked at my references, some from university lecturers, others from my own therapists who'd helped me recover from locked-in syndrome. Then there was a silence, followed by a few brief questions. I could see I wasn't the obvious choice. At last, (Marcos), one of my interviewers asked: "Peter, how many hours do you expect us to offer you? Assuming you're willing to consider a part-time position?" I decided honesty was the best policy.

"Listen Marcos, I'll tell it how it is," I replied. "I'm almost 40, I've lost my building career, lost my home, my wife, almost everything that mattered to me and I'm living in a garage on handouts from Centrelink trying to complete a course to help people. I've come through hell and fought my way through rehabilitation for almost six years. I've no professional experience to offer – but I do have lived experience, empathy and a need to help others, so if you give me just one hour a week to get my foot in the door, I promise I'll never let the company down." Another brief silence as the panel exchanged glances. They'd heard enough. "Okay, thank you, Peter. Could you leave the room for 5 minutes?"

By this stage, I'd convinced myself I was in the wrong place. "You're way over your head here, Pete!" and, as I waited, gazed at the pictures on the pinboard of support workers helping clients with different needs, all so competent, so highly professional. "How could I ever match up?" I thought, ruefully.

They called me in. "Peter, you have a very rare gift to give," said Marcos. "You have lived experience that few have to offer..." I sat there waiting for the inevitable "But." But the "But" never came!

"We have some clients with whom we feel you'll match very well," continued Marcos, "and we'd like to offer you a casual position for a 3-month probationary period. Does that sound fair?" Fair?!! I've never been so grateful for a job in all my life!

I've now been a support worker with the company for almost two years and have never missed one hour's work. I've gained skills in personal care, Down syndrome, Autism, behavioural issues, dementia, seniors' support and activity facilitation. Some of this experience was very daunting at first, but I still surprise myself with every new client. Of course, the company is selective on how much work I take on, and on matching me with clients too. Our service is tailored to individuals; each case has different needs for which another support worker may be better suited.

So now I had a job, and with my confidence renewed, I returned to my studies at TAFE. Because there was no system in place, when I first joined the course, the college lecturers were not sure how to pass me, as I had no work experience to speak of. After all the hard work

I'd put in during my initial semester, I didn't want another soul-destroying conversation this time!

Fortunately for me, Michelle Jenkins stepped in. Michelle is the CEO for Community Vision and a fearless leader; brought in to help build the company's strength ready for the NDIS – a government initiative which is set to transform Australia's care system, including Aged Care. After meeting with my lecturers, she arranged for an independent Occupational Therapist Assessor to come all the way from Armadale Hospital to the Woodvale Community Centre in the North of Perth. The lecturers agreed this was probably the only way they could pass me! Under Tania and Cathy's watchful and supporting eyes, I had to complete 140 hours of care management, they were the back bone behind that wonderful centre, thanks ladies. The tasks involved may sound easy, but they put me through my paces: assisting with running quizzes and bingo, serving at meal times and activities with dementia clients, that sort of thing, and assisting seniors to enjoy their time at the centre.

The OT Assessor was called Victoria. She observed how I connected with residents, my ability to run a small group by myself and also assist with larger groups. She seemed lovely (I've found 99% of OTs are) and filled me with such confidence that day! Of course, being watched made it hard to be my normal self, but Victoria was very positive. "As an Allied Health Assistant you either can or can't, you've either got it or you haven't. Today, Peter, I've seen the way the residents respond to you, and the kind manner you naturally have, so I've no problem passing you today. But…"

I braced myself for the inevitable criticism. "… I do think you should keep pushing yourself out of your comfort zone to grow in allied health." This was my last assessment to qualify. I'd passed! Yesssss!!!!

Thanks Michelle and Victoria! By now, I felt that I'd proved that, even with the worst kinds of stroke or ABIs, there's no limit to what you can achieve with persistence!

Chapter 44

With holding down a job these last few years, my rehabilitation has had to become a Friday thing; a 'Fix Pete Friday', as I told my company and they've supported me with that. I guess that means I'm a regular lad now, a thought that often hits me hard; sometimes I can sit and stare at nothing for hours on end, rather like some of the aged residents I cared for during my volunteer time at the home - just looking back in shock.

Life's strange because I'm stepping forward into a new life, as a new me! I still over-challenge myself and some friends tell me I need to slow down, which makes me smile. Because that means I'm still the old Pete too, still "giving it trainer!"

Life's not perfect, of course. Not long after I qualified, Mum was diagnosed with breast cancer. I must say, she handled it very calmly but then she's stronger than she looks, my Mum, coming through treatment with hardly a murmur. To cheer her up after her ordeal, I managed to get a small loan to take her on cruise from Fremantle, just down the coast. I think it worked! I was in the gym every morning (wouldn't you guess!) and was first for breakfast, beating 3,000 fellow passengers to the bacon!

I think the 4-day break did her good. Truth is, I couldn't really afford it, but you only get one Mum. Besides, I wanted to do just one positive thing, after putting her through hell since my stroke. Part of me wonders if the stress and worry of my illness contributed to hers, but she seems cancer-free now, touch wood!

Meanwhile, my rehabilitation continued. I managed to get a small rental near Mindarie Marina within walking distance of Surge Gym, where I met the most awesome personal trainer in Perth! At least to me! Warren offered to help me with my training techniques, to build more strength. Stubborn as I was when it came to training, I finally accepted some help. His motive was that he'd lost both of his parents to stroke when he was a kid and I know they'd be proud of him for helping me! "A free training session every *Fix Pete Friday!*" he promised; a course that lasted for several months and which I desperately needed, but could never have afforded. Wow! You don't get too many people like that in the world, ey! Even so, I tried to say "No, it's ok," but he just told me to shut up and "suck it up, Princess!" I swear I saw my Uncle Jim in him - his laugh was exactly the same! My Uncle Jim left this earth 20 odd years ago and I still miss him!

Warren (aka Wazza) certainly toughened me up! One of the hardest exercises was pushing the sled to extend the hips and knees and to strengthen my posterior chain. This actually worked wonders and had me breathing 'out of my arse', pushing up and down the gym like a rugby player, but I got results! And there were loads of different movements Warren introduced that I'd never heard of in my seven years' gym rehab, such as the 'farmer's carry walk'; walking with dumbbells to increase my grip and get me walking properly. Again, I got results.

Yep! Cheers, Wazza, "you're d' man!" He recently got a bronze medal on Perth's national stage, weighing in at 66.5 kg; not a big feller but he's bloody strong, able to squat 195kg, dead lift 217.5kg, and bench 112kg! That's tough! A true legend! And thanks to him, I'm stronger than ever!

It was coming...

Chapter 45

I knew every minute was valuable if I wanted to get back to ME, so I started to incorporate my rehab in everyday tasks. I found myself working out numbers like people do when trying to find money! Can we make the repayments on this loan? Well I had to find the minutes so I started calculating life!

They say an Englishman's answer to everything is a cup of tea! Well, actually the old *Tetley Extra Strong* did help this northern lad. I liked three cuppas on average most days but gave the sugar away. I worked out that six sugars a day equalled a wheelbarrow full per year! I started calculating life! Hold on Pete... three cups a day? That's 15 minutes kettle boiling time. I wonder what that is over a year or two? I can use this time. So I'd always try to do something, anything! Hold the counter and do heel raises mostly, or see if I can hold my arms out until the kettle clicked off. OUCH....THE BURN!!! I learned that you could work out doing any household task, even putting the tea bags on the next shelf up so you would struggle that little bit more!

I've also found trampolining a great challenge! Very, very, very big step and pretty scary at first! I remember walking into Aerial Trampoline World in Malaga, Perth. I got speaking to Rob the owner, he told me that he had a mild stroke years ago and trampolining fixed him! Well that was me... get me in there! There weren't many adults that day, mainly kids, but I didn't care. "Gotta do what ya gotta do," I thought. But, as I stepped onto the first trampoline, I realised very quickly, I couldn't even walk... Embarrassed, I rolled about the springing surface laughing, but I was actually in shock at how pathetic I felt! I tried desperately to get to my feet, yet every time I managed to get upright, a kid came bouncing past and the trampoline bounced me back on my arse again and I spent the next 30 minutes of my life on my back like a beetle! Eventually I crawled out, just, feeling damaged and having to realise how far I'd yet to go! Rob understood my embarrassing problem. "Just ring ahead next time you come, mate. When the kids are at school, you can virtually have the place to yourself." So I set my sights on half an hour a week at the quietest time! Thank goodness I persevered; otherwise I would never have learned the value of trampolining.

For the first month or so, just trying to get used to walking on that canvas or keeping my balance was an absolute mission and soooo difficult! I was still falling, but that's part of the exercise I guess, learning how to fall is just as important as trying to get up again. That springy surface, oh my God, what a nightmare after stroke!

The second month, I began to find my feet a bit and even managed to bounce on the surface. Trying to balance and bounce at the same time was exhausting, so much so I could hardly breathe at all but, even though I couldn't let my feet leave the trampoline, I had the up and down motion and Yay, I was upright! I thought back to coming with Jade and my cousin Amanda, on holiday from Leeds, when I could only watch from the sidelines as they had fun - Sad day! I never imagined that a few years later I'd be doing it myself.

About the same time as my trampolining, I also discovered the benefits of sweet potato which I'd eat 30 minutes before each session. Sweet potato is apparently one of the cleanest carbs you can get and, blended with bananas, is a terrific source of high carb protein; and, by adding Creatine powder to my water, I became a body builder! Yes, I qualify - I googled it! A body builder is "a person who strengthens and enlarges the muscles of their body through strenuous exercise." That's me!

Months later I was actually jumping on the trampoline - no flash moves breaking out - but my feet were leaving the canvas and I could jump around the square at least 10 times before I hit the deck, my breathing so deep it must have sounded like an asthma attack! By now, the value of trampolining had become very clear, involving every part of your body. It stretches your ham strings while intensely working your quadriceps and lifts the gluteus maximus to the max! With core strength, you have a better chance of lifting your arms and it works your respiratory system big time! Better speech and everything! Man! That place was a mission, but I will continue trampolining throughout my life now!

I heard a man on the radio say, "if we play like kids as adults, we set the benchmark of a much higher life span!" I truly believe that! Let's just say, if you last the full hour on a trampoline, you're pretty fit! Bet most people who try it for the first time will be shocked at how unfit they are!

Chapter 46

Well, I've pretty much shared with you all I can about my seven and half years' recovery. Currently, I'm a Community Board Member at Joondalup Jospital. I'm also working on a new design for a rehabilitation aid and most recently I have booked a flight to return to the Motherland - old Blighty - to challenge myself yet again in a way which only my roots can do! The mother of all stomping grounds, The Peak District in Derbyshire! I lived in Whaley Bridge for many years and know the Goyt Valley and surrounding peaks will push me to my limits, and then some!

My old mates are very supportive with offers of a room here and there, so I can travel at will. And I've booked a one-way ticket so that I can return when I'm ready.

An old army mate, Macca, has offered to train me in his boxing gym in Stockport. "Yo Adrian"... I... did... it!!!" Even a lad called Ash, who used to bully me at school, wants to walk the peaks with me, with his dog Jacko (a Border Collie).

To tell the truth, I am a little scared about doing such a big trip after everything, but I must step forward and start to live without fear of stroke! After all, I have a healthier lifestyle now, so I gotta think positive; I think I've proven the power of positivity and attitude with my story! And to any strokies or ABIs who are reading, I'd like to say this: "Although you'll hardly see your progress changing, I swear if you have persistence and commitment and it's relentless, then there can be change!" The truest saying I ever heard on my broken and often lonely road was, "Water cuts through rock, not because of its strength, but because of its persistence." That's bang on.

I believe my experience demonstrates the brain's incredible power to repair itself, to return from the brink of death and re-programme the body. If determination and human spirit exist, anything is possible.

And, no matter how humdrum life may seem, never, ever say you're 'bored'. Life can change, "In the blink of an eye".

"I CAN" and "I WILL" has got me this far and I hope my story can help someone, in some way, to never stop trying and never lose sight of the power of tomorrow!

I am Peter Coghlan whose life changed in 'A Blink of an Eye'. Today, I walk through life a new man – Reborn.

ACKNOWLEDGMENTS

Heartfelt thanks to:

Jade – we've travelled a long and difficult road together and I can never repay you for helping me and being my hope in those dark days when I struggled to hold on; no one could have given more.

Dr Scott Davies (Neuro-Radiology at Joondalup Hospital) - for removing the clot in my brain; without him, I would never have had the chance to fight and carry on with my life. He truly was a Godsend to me and I thank him from the bottom of my heart. I can't express the joy of my family and friends that I'm alive today. God Bless you, Dr Scott.

Professor Blacker and **Dr Steel** - for selecting me for rehabilitation; I am forever grateful and intend to complete the City to Surf with Dr Blacker some day, next time running side by side.

My sister **Vicky** - for believing in me and **Brad** (her husband) for the countless shaves and making me laugh. Vicky also helped save my life in my dying seconds at Joondalup A+E, by banging on a glass window and demanding help.

My **Dad** - for his words of encouragement and for fund-raising for Jade; when she was left without an income. Thanks also to his lovely wife **Noi** for all the massages and love she showed me on their visits.

My **Mum** - for homemade soup and tucking me in, feeding me at meal times with Jade - even though half ended up on whoever was doing it! For trying her best to meet any needs I had, as there were a fair few, and, with Jade's help, writing a list of my likes and dislikes, so the nurses could do their job.

Dave - for getting me to the hospital in time and saving my life! For looking after Jade throughout this nightmare and for doing things for me constantly now I am home. I must be a pain in the ass!

My **Uncle Peter** - for gardening and helping out around the place when no one else offered. Always willing and regularly checking up on me and Jade. Thanks mate!

Dan Hodson and his lovely wife **Andrea** - for making my videos and fund-raising for me and Jade, when we couldn't get any benefits due to immigration laws. And an extra thanks to Dan for phoning Jade every other day to console her and check on my progress. He's the best friend anyone could ever have and I love him like a brother.

Peter Evison (cakesolutions.net) – my lifelong friend. Thanks for you technical support.

Carolina Weightman (mougraphics.com) – for making my leaflets and 'release' video.

All the **amazing nurses** on my ward (too many to mention) - for the love and high level of care I received. For six months, you were my family, and I love you all! You lot rock!

All the therapists: **Speech, Occupational, Hydro** and, of course, my favourite – **Physio, Alisha**.

My **Auntie Eleanor** and **Uncle Alf** - for getting the Perth Hills together and raising money for Jade and myself in dark days indeed. For always being there, even when we had to have guarantors to stay in the country. Thanks so much.

Leroy and **Soda**, **Tracy** and **Carl**, **Julia** and **Sean**, **Noel** and **Gayle** and **Mark** - for yet another fund-raiser and for bringing their good friend **Tony McClusky** to play for me on my big release date. Greatly appreciated!

My good friend **Duncan Ogilvie** - who has helped me out financially over the past three years; words just can't express my gratitude for his continuing, unquestioning and generous support.

My **Nanna Marian, Grandad Derrick, Grandpop Robert, Uncle Jim** and all **my relatives** who have passed away, as I'm sure they were with me.

Thanks to **Edward and Victoria** (Form Designs Australia) - for helping me to get an idea off the ground, hopefully to help the World in my little way.

All **my friends and family** - who played a massive role in my recovery.

Almighty God himself - as I'm sure he's been there on my journey and continues to be so. I've never been religious, but now I'm open-minded, accepting that anything is possible - if only you believe.

And last, but by no means least, **Jacy Brean**. She is more than my 'ghost writer', she has truly been an angel; making sense of what I've said, helping me through emotionally very difficult times and sticking with me from the beginning, right to the very end. Jacy's help has made it possible for me to reach the people I want to. Thank you Jacy, from the bottom of my heart!